IDENTITY THEFT

How To Protect Your Most Valuable Asset

By
Robert J. Hammond, Jr.

CAREER PRESS

Franklin Lakes, NJ

IDENTITY THEFT

EDITED BY KATE PRESTON
TYPESET BY EILEEN DOW MUNSON
Cover design by Cheryl Cohan Finbow
Printed in the U.S.A. by Book-mart Press

Chapter 9 © Copyright 2000 - 2002, Identity Theft Resource Center, all rights reserved. Reprinted with permission.

Chapter 10 © Copyright March 2002, Identity Theft Resource Center, all rights reserved. Reprinted with permission

The Identity Theft IQ Test in chapter 6 was developed by the Privacy Rights Clearinghouse, *www.privacyrights.org*, and the Utility Consumers' Action Network, *www.ucan.org*. Used with permission of the Privacy Rights Clearinghouse.

To order this title, please call toll-free 1-800-CAREER-1 (NJ and Canada: 201-848-0310) to order using VISA or MasterCard, or for further information on books from The Career Press, Inc.

CAREER
PRESS

3 Tice Road, PO Box 687
Franklin Lakes, NJ 07417
www.careerpress.com

Library of Congress Cataloging-in-Publication Data
Hammond, Robert J.
    Identity theft : how to protect your most valuable asset / by Robert J. Hammond, Jr.
        p. cm.
    Includes index.
    ISBN 1-56414-636-7 (paper)
        1. False personation—United States. 2. False personation—United States—Prevention. I. Title.

    HV6679 H36 2003
    364.16'3—dc21

                                                    2002031593

WARNING

This publication is sold with the understanding that the author, publisher, and distributors of this book are not engaged in rendering legal, accounting or other professional services. If legal advice or other expert assistance is required, the services of a competent professional person should be sought.

This book contains certain sensitive information that could be easily subject to abuse or misuse. The author or publisher do not encourage, endorse or recommend the use of any of these methods as a means to defraud or violate the rights of any individual or organization.

The author, publisher, and distributors of this book hereby disclaim any responsibility for losses or liabilities allegedly caused by the use or misuse of any information presented herein. The book is presented for academic study and entertainment only.

In most cases, the names of victims and accused or convicted identity thieves have been changed. In some cases, occupations or locations have been altered as well.

37596 5-16-03

To all of the victims of identity theft and the unspoken heroes who serve us all.

————————

Thanks to my parents for teaching me the value of a good name.

Thanks to Ron Fry, Jackie Michaels, Michael Lewis, Kirsten Beucler, Jen Crespo, Stacey Farkas, Kate Preston, Anne Brooks, Briana Rosen, Brenda Brienza, Karen Wolf and the rest of the wonderful team at Career Press for working with me to make this book a great success.

Thanks to Norm Aladjem and Rick Berg of Writers and Artists Agency for teaching me the secret to working with Hollywood agents and entertainment lawyers.

Thanks to Lynn LoPucki, Security Pacific Bank Professor of Law at the UCLA School of Law, for his remarkable insights and controversial approach to the identity theft problem (see Appendix A).

Thanks to Stephen L. Carter, William Nelson Cromwell Professor of Law at Yale University, for being a positive role model.

Thanks to professors Brent F. Romney, Kevin A. Mohr, Laura R. Rovner, Greg Sergienko, Vivienne Alston, Stephanie Duran-Elie, Kristian Miccio, Todd Brower, Jennifer M. Russell, James A. Hayes, Jr., Terrence W. Roberts, and Amanda Gillespie, all at Western State University College of Law, for teaching me to analyze the facts, interpret the law, and put everything in writing.

Thanks to the Honorable Roger Luebs and the Cyber Crime Unit of the Riverside County District Attorney's Office for putting a serious dent in the rising occurrence of identity theft in Southern California and for providing help.

Thanks to Riverside County Chief Deputy District Attorney Michael Soccio for advising and encouraging me along the way.

Thanks to attorney/advocate Mari Frank; Beth Givens, Director of the Privacy Rights Clearinghouse; and Linda Foley, Director of the Identity Theft Resource Center, for their collective dedication to helping identity theft victims throughout the world.

Thanks to fellow writer and friend Brian Floyd for providing me with much-needed feedback as I prepared the early drafts.

Thanks to friend and scolar Carla Stalling-Huntington for being a true ally and mentor along this hero's journey.

Thanks to fellow author Mark Salzman for encouraging me to stay true to myself no matter what anybody else thinks and reminding me that it's okay to change directions at any time.

Thanks to master story teller Victor Villaseñor for showing me that the secret to great writing is rewriting.

Thanks to my tai chi ch'uan teacher, Sifu Harvey Kurland, for teaching me to remain balanced and centered as I brought this book into fruition.

Thanks to attorney John D. Woodward, Jr., Howard Beales of the FTC, and everyone else who helped make this book possible.

Table of Contents

Wake-up Call

RING!

Half awake, you hit the snooze button.

Riiinnnngggg!

The phone. The phone *is ringing. You glance at the clock. It's five a.m.!*

You're surprised when the unfamiliar voice asks for you by name. You're shocked at what he has to say.

"This is Mr. White from Cutthroat Collections Services. I'm calling about your past due account with Blue Sky Bank. Your account is three months in arrears and you need to make an immediate payment of $1762 or we will have to proceed with legal action against you."

You must be dreaming. You don't have *an account with Blue Sky Bank. You tell him so. The voice on the other end grows stern. "Our records indicate you have an outstanding credit card bill for $1762 which is more than three months overdue."*

"You've got the wrong person," you insist. "That's not my account." You hang up the phone and bury your face in the pillow.

Ten seconds later the phone rings again. You moan, then pick it up, reluctantly. It's him again.

"When can I expect payment?"

You hang up again. This time you turn off the ringer and try to go back to sleep. You toss and turn for an hour. When you finally get up to go to work, you ignore the blinking red message light on the phone.

When you arrive at work, there's a yellow Post-It Note on the middle of your desk. See your boss. Right away. Just as you head out the door, your phone rings. It's your bank. Your checking account is overdrawn. "That's impossible," you respond. "My last paycheck was direct-deposited just three days ago!" Instead of arguing, you tell the bank representative you'll call him back later.

When you enter the boss's office, she tells you, pokerfaced, that you were being considered for a promotion. "Finally," you think, "some good news!" As you begin to thank her, she interrupts you and reemphasizes the word were, which you must have missed the first time around. She's sorry, but a routine background check revealed a number of delinquent accounts, at least three judgements against you...and some kind of trouble with the law.

"As a result," she declares, and now her look and voice are positively icy, "you are not getting the promotion. We simply can't trust you anymore. In fact, you are terminated, effective immediately."

You start to protest, but two beefy security guards appear at the door. They hand you a cardboard box and stand, glaring, as you clear out your desk. You feel your co-workers' cold stares as you shamble down the hall.

You step outside into the morning cold and walk toward the lot where your car is parked. Yep, there it is, hitched to a tow truck! "Wait," you yell at the driver. "Stop! You're making a mistake."

He flicks a cigarette out the window in your direction and snarls, "That's what they all say." He pulls away quickly, leaving you standing there on the corner panting for breath.

OK, *you tell yourself,* this is just a really bad day. Calm down. Call someone.

You try your cell phone. It doesn't work. No dial tone. Nothing. You cross the street to a pay phone. Your best friend, Beth, agrees to meet you at a nearby deli.

You pour out your tale of woe over a tuna melt as Beth listens sympathetically. She offers to pay for the meal, but you insist on picking up the check. You hand the cashier your Visa Gold card. He runs it through the machine. You wait for what seems like hours before the red LCD blinks: DECLINED. You offer up another card. DECLINED. You look through your wallet for cash or another credit card. Beth drops a twenty on the counter and tells the cashier to keep the change as she gently guides you to the door.

On the drive home, Beth tries to give you a couple of twenties. You push her hand away.

"It's OK. I'll be fine. I just need to make a couple of calls to clear stuff up. Something really weird is happening."

As you step from the car, you hear the thumping sound of a helicopter circling low overhead. Then you're engulfed in sirens and surrounded by flashing red and blue lights. A policeman, with gun drawn, orders you to lie face down on the ground. Your arms are twisted behind your back. You feel the steel tightening around your wrists, the weight of a man's knee in the middle of your back.

"You're under arrest," a burly cop snaps. "You have the right to remain silent. Anything you say can be held against you. You have the right to an attorney. Should you not be able…"

You see Beth standing next to her car, a man in a dark suit whispering to her. She looks at you and nods. When your eyes meet, she quickly glances away. Suddenly you wonder if she's part of the whole thing. Wait, what thing? What the heck is going on?

"You've got the wrong guy! It isn't me! It isn't me! Doesn't anybody understand? What's wrong with all you people?"

Two cops drag you, kicking and screaming, and toss you into the back seat of a patrol car, nearly slamming the door on your foot. What was it one of the cops said? Armed robbery?

You?

It's nine o'clock in the morning, and your life has been lost. Actually, it's been stolen.

You are a victim of identity theft.

But who's going to believe you?

Who did this to you?

How are you going to prove your innocence?

Most of all, how are you going to get your life back? At least, whatever's left of it.

The answers lie ahead.

Introduction

What's Your Name Worth?

"A good name is rather to be chosen than great riches."

—Proverbs 22

What's the most important thing you own? The most valuable? So valuable that losing it would have a devastating effect on your life, not just emotionally but financially?

Your house? Your car? Bank accounts? Your collections of coins, stamps, rare books, art?

While having any of these stolen or even damaged could be a traumatic experience, you're probably insured against their outright loss. Your house would be repaired, your car paid for, collections could be replaced or at least compensated for.

But what about what sets you apart from everyone else— your good name? What if somebody stole it? What would you do if someone else were suddenly...*you?*

This year, identity thieves will defraud nearly a million Americans. Using methods as basic as picking through garbage and as sophisticated as mining computer databases through-out the world, a phalanx of imposters may be targeting *you* and everything you own, right now. If they are successful, they could max-out your credit cards, wipe out your bank accounts, apply for (and max-out) *new* credit cards, even new loans, *in your name*. Worse, they could sell your house, buy and sell just about anything else you can think of (*in your name*), put you into bankruptcy, even commit crimes...while masquerading as *you*.

And you probably wouldn't even know it's going on until it's much too late. How do you know that someone else isn't using your identity right now?

You don't.

And what's your good name *really* worth anyway? Well, as an article written by Kristin Davis, in *Kiplinger's Personal Finance* magazine, put it: "You may think your good name is invaluable, but on the street it sells for about $25."[1]

Identity Theft: How to Protect Your Most Valuable Asset is the most effective tool in your arsenal against the identity crook. Learn how to protect your identity—while you still have one.

This book will show you how identity theft—the fastest growing crime in America—affects every one of us and what to do about it. All of us are fair game for the predatory identity thief.

Think you're immune? Think again.

◆ Have you reviewed your credit reports—from all three of the major reporting agencies—within the last six months?

◆ Do you shred all of your personal papers, receipts, old utility bills, and pre-approved credit card offers before you toss them in the trash?

◆ Do you keep your social security card in a safe place, not in your wallet or purse?

◆ Have you had your name and address removed from mailing lists for pre-approved credit card offers by "opting out?"

If you answered no to any of the previous questions, your identity may already be compromised. Someone may already be using your name and Social Security number to run up thousands of dollars worth of credit and bad check charges, leaving you with a mountain of debt, or perhaps even the subject of arrest warrants.

This book is written for anyone who wants to protect their most valuable asset from the plundering of identity thieves. It is also designed to help the millions of individuals who have already been victimized. It will show you how to avoid being a victim and how to fight and win back your good name.

It is also a wake-up call to business owners, corporate executives, government policymakers, legal professionals, and law enforcement personnel—all of whom must be involved in crafting effective solutions to a growing problem.

In addition to providing a practical step-by-step approach to prevention, protection, personal recovery, and policy-making, *Identity Theft* brings you an inside look at the individual lives that are effected and devastated by this far-reaching epidemic. You'll also get a look inside the minds and lives of the identity thieves themselves. You will learn their methods, their motivations, and where their money goes.

Best of all, you will discover little-known ways to ensure you and your family aren't just helpless sheep waiting to be slaughtered. You will be able to rebuild and maintain your credit rating and personal assets without living in fear or ignorance.

I encourage you to share the ideas in this book with your friends, family, co-workers, employees, and local representatives. Each of us can make a difference in solving this devastating problem. Then, we can work together to end this growing epidemic—once and for all.

Chapter

The Extent of the Problem

"I mean, think of how easy it is...You go to a restaurant...You sign the bill. You use a credit card. Your credit card number is on the duplicate. What happens with the duplicate? Somebody picks it up. They've got your name, they've got a credit card number, and they're kind of off to the races."[1]

—Sen. Diane Feinstein

In a 1999 *Wall Street Journal* poll, Americans claimed the loss of privacy was their greatest fear, beating out terrorism, global warming and overpopulation, among other contenders.

A 2000 Lou Harris poll found that nearly 90 percent of people were concerned about threats to their privacy, an increase from only 34 percent in 1970. Those polled were nearly unanimous (94 percent) in their beliefs that personal information was vulnerable to misuse. And more than three quarters of them admitted they had declined to answer questions from a business because they thought they were "too personal."

People have good reason to fear. The information explosion, aided by an decade of easy credit, has led to the exponential expansion of a crime that feeds on the inability of consumers to control who has access to sensitive information and how it is safeguarded. That crime is identity theft.

"...[T]he stories in the news on identity theft are not extreme cases in which an unlucky victim has had an unusually bad experience. As one victim from California stated, 'It was as terrible as all the books and articles say it is.'"[2]

They are everywhere

Identity thieves don't need to storm a bank vault, pistol whip a convenience store clerk or try to sell you worthless stock to steal your money. All they have to do is find a way to get a *little* information—your name, Social Security number, address, date of birth, credit card number, cell phone number. They don't even need *most* of that information, let alone all of it. A Social Security number will work just fine, thank you. An identity thief's gold mine is simply the sum total of your everyday transactions.

Purchasing gasoline, meals, clothes, home-improvement tools, or tickets to an athletic event; renting a car or a video; purchasing gifts or trading stock online; receiving mail; taking out the garbage—*any activity in which identity information is shared or made available to others creates an opportunity for identity theft.*[3]

Identity theft has been referred to by some as the crime of the new millennium. It can be accomplished anonymously, easily, with a variety of means, and the impact upon the victim can be devastating. Since time immemorial, criminals had to sucker their victims face to face. Identity theft requires no direct communication between criminal and victim. Simply doing things that are part of your everyday routine may give identity thieves enough of an opportunity to get unauthorized access to personal data and commit identity theft.[4]

In one notorious case of identity theft, the criminal, a convicted felon, not only incurred more than $100,000 of credit card debt, obtained a federal home loan, and bought homes, motorcycles, and handguns in the victim's name, but called his victim to taunt him…before filing for bankruptcy…in the victim's name. While the victim and his wife spent more than four years and $15,000 of their own money to restore their credit and reputations, the criminal served a brief sentence for making a false statement to procure a firearm, but made no restitution to his victims for any of the harm he had caused.[5]

In many cases, unsuspecting victims have no idea that anything has even happened until they start getting dunned by high-decibel bill collectors or have trouble applying for a job, loan, or mortgage. They then discover that their credit has been seriously damaged or even ruined by any number of purchases undertaken in their name by the impersonator. In what may be the worst possible scenario for victims of identity theft, the impersonator may commit a separate criminal act, resulting in the victim actually facing criminal charges for a crime committed by an imposter.[6]

Victims of identity theft face an enormous and arduous task in repairing both their credit rating and their emotional well being. One of the biggest obstacles they face is that they are, more or less, completely on their own. The prevailing attitude of most creditors advised of a case of identity fraud is downright skepticism. Most creditors require identity-theft victims to submit an affidavit testifying that they did not incur the debt themselves. Many creditors may require more, including the submission of copies of the victim's driver's license, Social Security card, or birth certificate. Understandably, many victims already sucked into the quagmire of identity theft are not eager to hand over these personal identification items, particularly since many victims suspect that a creditor's negligence probably led to the identity theft in the first place![7]

According to Riverside County Judge Roger Luebs, formerly head of the Cyber Crime Unit of the Riverside County District Attorney's Office, identity thieves come in all shapes and sizes, "from petty thieves and junkies to doctors and business executives. Some people are living very well using the credit worthiness and identities of other people."[8]

The statistics are scary...and getting worse

▸ In fiscal year 1999 alone, the Social Security Administration (SSA) Office of Inspector General (OIG) Fraud Hotline received approximately 62,000 allegations involving SSN misuse.[9]

▸ A 1998 General Accounting Office (GAO) report ("Identity Fraud: Information on Prevalence, Cost, and Internet Impact is Limited") revealed that in 1995, 93 percent of arrests made by the U.S. Secret Service Financial Crimes Division involved identity theft. In 1996 and 1997, 94 percent of financial crimes arrests involved identity theft. The Secret Service stated that actual losses to individuals and financial institutions totaled $442 million in 1995, $450 million in 1996, and $745 million in 1997.

▸ Postal Inspection investigations revealed that a significant portion of identity fraud was undertaken by organized crime syndicates, especially to support drug trafficking, and had a nationwide scope.

▸ Trans Union Corporation, one of the three major national credit bureaus, stated that two-thirds of its consumer inquiries to its fraud victim department involved identity fraud. Such inquiries had increased from an average of less than 3,000 a month in 1992 to more than 43,000 a month in 1997.

▶ VISA USA and MasterCard International both stated that overall fraud losses from their member banks were in the hundreds of millions of dollars annually. MasterCard stated that dollar losses relating to identity fraud represented about 96 percent of its member banks' overall fraud losses of $407 million in 1997.[10]

▶ A new FTC hotline (877-IDTHEFT) is already logging more than 3,000 calls a week...and most people don't even know it exists. The FTC reported more than a fourfold increase in identity theft complaints between November, 1999 and March, 2001.

▶ An independent study in 1999 commissioned by Image Data LLC, an identity theft prevention service, found that approximately one out of every five Americans, or a member of their families, have been victimized by identity theft.

▶ According to James Huse Jr., the inspector general of the Social Security Administration, a preliminary investigation found that as many as one in 12—or more than 100,000 of the 1.2 million foreigners obtaining new Social Security numbers—illegally use fake documents to get the cards.

▶ A study commissioned by Identico Systems, a maker of electronic-fraud detection devices, estimated that identity thieves had victimized 13 percent of Americans. Compare that to the national robbery rate, which, according to the U.S. Bureau of Justice Statistics, stood at 0.32 percent in 2000.

▶ And in a May, 2000 study jointly published by the California Public Interest Research Group (CALPIRG and the Privacy Rights Clearinghouse, "[l]ess than half of the respondents felt that their cases had been fully resolved, and those with unsolved cases had been dealing with the problem for an average of four years. Victims estimated that they spent an average of 175 hours and $808 in additional out-of-pocket costs to fix the problems stemming from identity theft."[11]

It took those who *had* solved their cases nearly two years to do so. Total fraudulent charges averaged $18,000, but were as high as $200,000.[12]

It's so easy, so doggone easy

Despite your best efforts to manage the flow of your personal information or to keep it to yourself, skilled identity thieves may use a variety of methods, from the most banal to the most sophisticated, to gain access to your data. Here are just some of the ways identified by the FTC that imposters can get your personal information and take over your identity:

- ◆ They steal wallets and purses containing your identification and credit and bankcards.

- ◆ They steal your mail, including your bank and credit card statements, pre-approved credit offers, telephone calling cards and tax information.

- ◆ They complete a "change of address form" to divert your mail to another location.

- ◆ They rummage through your trash, or the trash of businesses, for personal data in a practice known as "dumpster diving."

- ◆ They fraudulently obtain your credit report by posing as a landlord, employer, or someone else who may have a legitimate need for—and a legal right to—the information.

- ◆ They get your business or personnel records at work.

- ◆ They find personal information in your home.

- ◆ They use personal information you share on the Internet.

◆ They buy your personal information from "inside" sources. For example, an identity thief may pay a store employee for information about you that appears on an application for goods, services or credit.[13]

Once they've gotten it, here are just some of the ways they can use your personal information:

◆ They call your credit card issuer and, pretending to be you, ask to change the mailing address on your credit card account. The imposter then runs up charges on your account. Because your bills are being sent to the new address, it may take some time before you realize there's a problem.

◆ They open a new credit card account, using your name, date of birth, and SSN. When they use the credit card and don't pay the bills, the delinquent account is reported on your credit report.

◆ They establish phone or wireless service in your name.

◆ They open a bank account in your name and write bad checks from that account.

◆ They file for bankruptcy under your name to avoid paying debts they've incurred under your name, or to avoid eviction.

◆ They counterfeit checks or debit cards, and drain your bank account.

◆ They buy cars by taking out auto loans in your name.[14]

There's no single way, no simple path. Identity thieves are nothing if not creative, even brazen, in their methods. Attorney

General John Ashcroft highlighted a few of the most egregious examples of this "creativity" in a May, 2002, press conference:

"One case involved defendants who located houses owned by elderly citizens and assumed their identities in order to sell or refinance, fraudulently, the properties.

"One defendant is charged with selling Social Security numbers on eBay.

"One hospital employee allegedly stole the identities of 393 hospital patients to obtain credit cards using the false identities.

"Another individual is charged with stealing the identity of a company executive and selling 176,000 of that executive's stock shares."[15]

And in Chicago, a man allegedly committed murder to effect a switch of his identity with the murder victim. This case deserves some detail. J.P. was ready to plead guilty to operating an extensive document-counterfeiting ring that, for a fee, provided counterfeit birth certificates, fraudulently obtained Social Security cards, and Illinois driver's licenses to more than 100 individuals.

Four days before he was due in court, J.P. allegedly killed a homeless man in order to fake his own death, avoid prosecution, and escape unnoticed. He had reportedly made arrangements with a local crematorium to have his body cremated in the event of his death and then recruited another person to "find a body" of someone who "looked like" him, suggesting soup kitchens and the Salvation Army as potential trolling places. Why there? Because the police would never look for someone "like that" if the person was missing.

According to the U.S. Attorney's Office, the two of them suffocated the homeless man that day in J.P.'s apartment. Ever resourceful, J.P. had conveniently arranged for the Chicago

Fire Department to come to his apartment, where, of course, they found the "replacement" body, which was transferred to the crematorium under J.P.'s name.

Federal authorities managed to reach the crematorium before the body was cremated. Given that the homeless victim weighed only 165 pounds and J.P. tipped the scales at more than 450 pounds (and "J.P." was not wearing the electronic monitoring ankle bracelet that the district court had ordered him to wear), they discovered the ruse.

J.P. was eventually captured in Boston and indicted with seven co-defendants (including his brother, sister, niece, and personal physician).[16]

If that didn't make you want to immediately cut up every credit card you own and swear to never talk to a telemarketer again, the next two chapters will *really* scare you. They describe, sometimes in excruciating detail, dozens of cases of identity theft, from the simple and relatively "cheap" to the most bizarre and disturbing, the latter involving far more than just a loss of money.

Chapter

2

Confessions of an Identitiy Thief

By Carson James

In the time it takes you to watch the latest episode of "ER," I can run up more than $20,000 in bad debts in *your* name and disappear without a trace. You may not even realize that you have your own "emergency" until you apply for a loan or try to refinance your house...and the lender turns you down because your credit's no good. Or until bill collectors start making threatening phone calls and shouting obscenities about debts you know nothing about.

Who am I?

I'm that bum digging through the dumpster behind your place of employment. You probably thought I was just collecting cans, didn't you?

I'm an insurance clerk or bank employee with easy access to all of your personal data. I can access your credit rating without your knowledge and at my leisure so I can decide whether your information is worth stealing.

I'm a high-tech cyber hacker who can tap into your bank's computer to check your balances and credit limits and print out a list of your account numbers and passwords for sale to the highest bidder.

I'm a coworker with access to your personnel records, including your employment application, payroll data and, of course, your Social Security number.

I'm that woman you met at a bar one night. You took me home, wondered why I never called you, then realized you knew nothing about me and had no way of finding me again. And you never even noticed that an old bank statement was missing.

I'm the long-lost friend you saw at your high school reunion who spent the night reminiscing about the good old days.

I'm your next-door neighbor.

I'm your sibling.

I'm your parent.

I'm your child.

In other words, I could be just about anybody. And with very little effort, I can become *you*.

How we operate

Most of the people I know in this business fall into one of several categories.

First are the opportunists, usually those in a position of trust—relatives, friends or coworkers. He or she may be experiencing temporary financial pressures or simply succumb to temptation when an opportunity presents itself.

An acquaintance of mine (I'll call him Oscar) fell into an unexpected opportunity when his wealthy uncle offered to sign him up with a network marketing company. The application contained the uncle's Social Security number. Oscar, who happened to have a severe drug problem at the time, decided he could make faster money than the company could ever offer just by using his uncle's Social Security number to apply for a credit card. It was just going to be temporary, Oscar promised himself. He was just going to use the credit card—*one* credit card—until he could get back on his feet. And since he planned to pay the minimum due every month, without fail, he figured his uncle would never even know what he'd done.

Three months later, Oscar had five credit cards with a combined limit of $50,000—all in his uncle's name—and all charged to the max. Despite his best intentions, Oscar's drug habit got the best of him, and he started to fall behind in the payments. Eventually, he stopped making payments altogether.

His uncle didn't find out until six months later, when a bank turned him down for a business loan because of the five delinquent accounts on his credit report. By the time the uncle figured out what happened, Oscar was doing a two-year prison stint on unrelated drug and weapons charges. It took the uncle nearly a year to reestablish his good name. Oscar, of course, never paid him or the credit card companies a dime.

Then there's the story of Jane Z. and Cat McKenzie. In her late-20s, Jane seemed to have it all. A former beauty queen, she was a smart college graduate, fluent in five languages, and spoiled rotten by her rich French boyfriend. Until the day he decided it was time to "trade her in" for a younger model.

Before she split, Jane swiped one of his gold cards and went on a big spending spree. It was, she felt, a well-deserved reward for putting up with the two-timing jerk who dumped her. Jane never meant to become an identity thief, but the ex-boyfriend pressed charges. She got six months in jail for her misdeeds.

While locked up, Jane met Cat Girl McKenzie, whose nickname reflected her athletic prowess...and uncanny ability to scale high-rise luxury buildings. After climbing them, she was also quite skilled at sneaking in and out of luxury hotels, townhouses, and executive suites without leaving a trace. Going from room to room, or apartment to apartment, she would steal information from the inhabitants' personal papers and computer files while they were eating, watching television or even sleeping in the next room. Armed with stacks of passwords, Social Security numbers, driver's license information, account numbers and the like, she'd drain the victims' existing accounts, then open up new accounts and run *those* into the ground...all in a matter of days. The owners never knew what hit them until months later, by which time, of course, Cat Girl was long gone.

Cat Girl taught Jane how to stay out of trouble while in jail and how to make a fortune when she got out. The pair hooked up when they both made bail and started running identity-theft scams across the country while hanging out with the jet-setting rich-and-famous set. Jane would use her good looks and charm to pick up wealthy businessmen. While they wined and dined her, Cat Girl would sneak into their homes or offices and copy down all the information she could find. The two would then use the compromised credit cards to purchase whatever they knew they could quickly sell and drain every bank account they could locate.

One day, they tried to scam an undercover government agent who had gotten wind of their little game and set up a sting operation. In exchange for reduced sentences, Cat Girl and Jane agreed to work as undercover agents themselves for a multi-agency government task force specializing in identity theft and white-collar crime.

Dumpster divers create their own opportunities. Usually low-life junkies and ex-cons, they root through garbage cans looking for employment and credit applications thrown out by businesses or pre-approved credit offers and receipts tossed out by residents from nice neighborhoods. Sometimes they'll just sell the information they find to a professional credit thief or forgery ring, which will, in turn, establish checking and credit accounts in the stolen names. Depending on the "quality" of these names and corresponding information, each name will fetch anywhere from $10 to $50. A good diver can easily support a $200-a-day crack habit just by going though people's garbage. Which, I guess, gives new meaning to the phrase, "One man's trash is another man's treasure."

Sometimes dumpster divers work in teams as part of a larger identity-theft ring. In other cases, they set up the identities themselves and go on a spending spree until they burn out a name, then start over with the next victim.

Which is pretty much the story of habitual criminal Felix H., who got out of prison one morning with nothing but the $200 "gate money" the Department of Corrections gives to parolees.

As soon as he got into town, Felix dug through a couple of dumpsters in a commercial area until he found a stack of discarded job applications. He found the name of a systems analyst and paid less than $100 for a counterfeit Social Security card and driver's license—with his picture and the victim's name. An hour later, Felix headed to a local bank and opened a checking account with his remaining $100 and new identification papers.

He then proceeded to the local motorcycle shop and bought himself a brand-new Harley, using the victim's credit references, of course. Later that evening, he used the victim's account numbers—which he obtained in a few minutes by downloading a free credit report off the Internet—and charged over $50,000 in saleable merchandise and cash advances. By the end of the day, Felix was riding his new Harley off into the sunset—on to another day in the life of an identity thief. The poor systems analyst will probably spend the next two years trying to get his credit record cleared.

Higher up the identity theft food chain are the techno geek hacker types. Most of these propeller heads can steal an entire company's database or pull a hundred thousand records from a credit bureau in a matter of minutes. Often they'll sell blocks of names with "gold balls" credit to the highest bidder. They frequent underground computer bulletin boards, chat rooms and hacker conventions, buying and selling credit card numbers, names, Social Security numbers and batches of A-1 credit reports by the hundreds.

I suppose you're wondering when I'm going to get to my own story. This is supposed to be a confession, after all. Ok, here goes.

It's confession time

Like most crooks, I didn't exactly wake up one day and proclaim, "I think I'm going to steal people's identities for a living. Yeah, that's the ticket."

I came from a good home with good parents in a good neighborhood and I went to good schools. I play the violin and a pretty good game of chess. I went to a decent college and worked for a couple of Fortune 500 companies. So where did I go wrong?

I wish I could blame the problems of my life on childhood abuse, bad parents, poverty, or social deprivation. Unfortunately, I have nobody to blame but myself. I made poor choices. I got greedy. I looked for the easy way to get what I wanted. What more can I say?

When asked why he robbed banks, the infamous Willie Sutton supposedly replied, "because that's where the money is." Well, the target's the same, but the biggest robbers today don't need to use guns or threats. They can use computers. The average bank robber may be lucky to get away with $5,000... and face a 10-year prison sentence if he's caught.

Using a computer, smart identity thieves can withdraw more than 10 times that amount on a daily basis, without leaving a trace. No hidden cameras. No clues. No fingerprints. No witnesses. No crime partners to rat them out when they get caught. In most cases the crime isn't even discovered until months later.

I started out with a list of 10 names and Social Security numbers I purchased for $500 from an information broker. "These names are as good as gold," he promised me, then told me how I could use them to apply for credit online, open checking accounts, or buy new cars. So I gave it a shot.

I used three of the names to apply for online credit cards and open bank accounts.

I used five others to set up phony companies with merchant accounts so they could accept credit card payments.

I used the last two names to open offshore bank accounts where I transferred the money from the phony companies after the credit card charges from the purchaser accounts cleared the merchant accounts. During the next month, I wired the money from one bank to the next, then closed out all of the accounts after withdrawing over $100,000—cash. Not bad for a $500 initial investment, I thought. I repeated the process, this time with 100 names. And so it went...

I used most of the cash to purchase investment-grade gold and silver coins. They were easy to liquidate, nearly impossible to trace, and highly portable—you can literally hold $1 million in the palm of your hand, put it in your pocket and fly down to the Cook Islands for a weekend vacation. (On July 30, 2002, a 1933 Saint Gaudens Double Eagle sold for $7.59 million at Sotheby's in New York.)

I did all of my business online, so I never had to produce any photo ID, leave a signature or subject myself to video surveillance. I kept all of my transactions under $10,000 to avoid federal reporting requirements. I never used an identity for more than a week. I maintained as many as 50 different bank accounts around the world in the names of just as many individuals, corporations, and trusts. I closed most accounts within a month and reopened new ones so as not to leave a trail.

Then came 9/11. I knew the Feds would be cracking down big time on all electronic financial transactions and offshore transfers. Identity theft is one of the primary ways the terrorists funded their weapons purchases, training camps, flight schools, and related activities.

So, I did what any self-respecting thief would do—I went for one final big score. Unfortunately, it really was final. Apparently, the information broker I worked with had been caught in a nationwide sweep for money laundering and a long list of other financial crimes. In return for leniency, he gave the FBI all of his records, including information that implicated me in hundreds of cases of identity theft, money laundering, and fraud. My lawyer told me I would be lucky to get anything less than 20 years in federal prison. Since my only co-conspirator was the information broker who had given me up, they didn't offer me any deals.

So I offered them a deal—in exchange for probation with no prison time, I would give them a full confession and make complete and immediate financial restitution to all the victims.

Well, I only got 10 years and might be out in five. It's really not so bad. So you can feel safe for a little while. But when I get out, I'm going to need some money. Have any?

Don't worry, I'll just help myself. You won't even know I've been there...for a while, anyway.

Chapter

Gypsters, Trash, and Thieves

R.C. and K.W. were two losers from Vermont bored with their small-town lives. They settled on Australia as a fanciful destination. Lacking plane fare (or, for that matter, brains), they crafted a simple plan: They would kill someone, steal his ATM cards and PIN numbers, and loot his accounts to raise travel money. Posing as students conducting a survey, they attacked and killed two university professors who were unlucky enough to be home when they knocked. K.W. was sent away for 25 years; R.C. got life.[1]

These guys were obviously young and stupid. Why kill someone to get an ATM card? They could have gotten everything they needed—and more money than they ever dreamed of—with a lot less work, a lot less heartache, and a lot less jail time.

Here are just a few true stories that prove how surprisingly easy it is to take over someone's identity and rob them blind in a matter of days, if not hours.

A hairy encounter

While applying to rent an apartment, M.R. saw other completed applications lying on a nearby table. When the manager left the room for a moment, M.R. quickly hid them among his own papers. After M.R. left the complex, the apartment manager noticed the applications were missing. Fortunately, he still had the applicants' phone numbers in a separate log, so he immediately called to notify them that their applications had been stolen. But before anyone could do anything, M.R. had used the information on the applications to obtain half a dozen credit cards, a business line of credit for his hair salon, and $300,000 worth of fixtures for his shop.

After his arrest, investigators discovered M.R. was also using the identification papers of a dead person to apply for even more credit cards and those of another individual whose wallet he had stolen a few weeks earlier. M.R. was eventually charged with 60 counts of identity theft and fraud.[2]

A little bit me, a little bit you

In July 1999, F.S., of Chula Vista, California, was sentenced to 16 months in federal prison for using a stolen Social Security number to obtain thousands of dollars in credit and then filing for bankruptcy (in the name of her victim) after defaulting on the loans.

The victim, whose name was similar to F.S.'s, had graduated from a college in Arizona that F.S. also briefly attended. Both women had received student loans that were administered by the same company. Through a computer mix-up, documents belonging to the victim—which included her Social Security number—were sent to F.S. Shortly thereafter, the victim began receiving telephone calls from companies she had never heard of claiming she owed them large sums of money.

F.S., who was a notary public and had been employed as a paralegal, could not resist the opportunity the college's error afforded her.[3]

Where there's an opportunity...

Sometimes we all make it so easy for identity thieves to operate, *we* should be the ones charged with a crime.

When various people who picked up their mail at a U.S. post office threw away merchandise catalogs, which, of course, contained their names and account numbers, a woman went through the trash, removed the catalogs, and used the identifying information to order merchandise in other people's names.[4]

J.H.'s employment regularly took her away from home for extended periods of time. At some point, another woman began using her name, Social Security number, and educational and professional licensing information. She took out loans for real property and vehicles in J.H.'s name, even obtained a professional license and employment in J.H.'s field.

The woman failed to repay the loans, and ultimately filed for bankruptcy...using J.H.'s name and Social Security number. J.H. didn't find out about the long-standing fraud until she returned from an overseas work assignment and discovered that her credit was virtually destroyed.[5]

Let your fingers do the walking

Sometimes just one small piece of information, properly exploited, can help an identity thief build an entire dossier on a brand-new victim.

One case currently under investigation by the FBI and U.S. Postal Service involves someone who obtained the names and dates of birth of Boston-area attorneys just by copying the *Martindale-Hubbell Law Directory*.

Using this information, a cohort visited the Massachusetts Bureau of Vital Records, which has an open records policy, and obtained copies of birth certificates of potential victims.

Using *that* information, the two contacted the Social Security Administration, obtained the victims' Social Security numbers and ordered credit reports from one of the bureaus. All of which gave them more than enough information to determine the creditworthiness of each prospective victim and identify existing bank and credit card accounts.

Using the information of just one victim, they managed to get his bank to wire transfer $96,000 out of one of his accounts. They also added authorized users to the victims' credit card accounts and ordered emergency replacement cards, which were sent to them by overnight delivery by the ever-vigilant credit card companies.

At least 12 different licenses or identification cards from three states and numerous credit cards—all in the names of the victims whose identities had been stolen—were recovered when they were arrested.[6]

Terrorist connections

Though identity theft is usually a monetary crime, its use in the 9/11 attacks is a frightening example of how extreme the results can be.

You probably remember the FBI's confusing declarations after 9/11. Within days, the 19 men responsible for the hijackings and destruction of the World Trade Center had been identified. Or were they? In a very short time, the same FBI officials who had appeared so confident admitted that they weren't really sure about some of those identifications. At least seven of the named suicide hijackers, it seemed, were still very much alive, victims of identity theft.[7]

"Everyone agreed this was a new wrinkle," said Joanna Crane of the Federal Trade Commission. "...These guys had done what's called an 'identity takeover', living completely under the name of another person, with drivers' licenses, passports, bank accounts, phone accounts—everything that identifies you." It was all too easy for them live openly, for years, under other identities.[8]

A new wrinkle, but far from an isolated case: Speaking before Congress in July 2002, Dennis Lormel, chief of the FBI's Terrorist Financial Review Group, revealed that a recently busted Al Qaeda cell in Spain used stolen credit cards in fictitious sales scams and for numerous other purchases for the cell. They also used stolen telephone and credit cards to stay in touch with accomplices in Pakistan, Afghanistan, and Lebanon. Extensive use of false passports and travel documents were used to open bank accounts so money could also be sent to and from those countries.[9]

"The methods used to finance terrorism range from the highly sophisticated to the most basic. There is virtually no financing method that has not, at some level, been exploited by these people," Lormel testified. "Identity theft is a key catalyst fueling many of these methods."[10]

Most of these methods, especially the basic, wouldn't be so effective if reasonable controls were in place. But even when they are, lazy or uncaring overseers can make a terrorist's job surprisingly easy. The FBI's Lormel revealed that the September 11 hijackers opened three dozen bank accounts without having *any* legitimate Social Security numbers. In some cases, they brazenly jotted down a series of random numbers in lieu of real Social Security numbers. They would have been caught, of course, if anyone had bothered to check the numbers. No one did.

And the hijackers had a lot of outside help—others ready to commit identity theft on their behalf. On January 14, 2002, the FBI arrested Mohamed Amry, a 36-year-old Algerian. According to the criminal complaint, Amry, who worked as a personal trainer at a Bally's Fitness Club in Massachusetts, "sold the names and Social Security numbers of 21 members of Bally's...that were used to create phony passports, citizenship papers, and credit cards, and to open bank accounts in Boston and New York City that were used to cash counterfeit checks."

The recipient of Amry's stolen identities was "linked" to al Qaeda at the time, but was, in fact, later convicted of being part of the "Millennium Bomb Plot." His target? Los Angeles International Airport.[11]

Another helper, Mohamad El Atriss, was arrested in August 2002, as he stepped off a flight from Cairo. Two of the thousands of fake IDs he produced in Paterson, New Jersey, became part of the 9/11 terrorist plot—one was carried by Khalid Almihdhar, whose hijacked plane plowed into the Pentagon; the other went to Abdul Aziz Alomari, one of the hijackers on Flight 11, which hit the north tower of the World Trade Center.[12]

This was the same Atriss who had left for Egypt a month earlier—just hours before his home and businesses were raided by local police and the FBI. The hero of the story was a Minnesota company from which he tried to buy a sophisticated copier that would have enabled him to emboss seals, like those used on official state and Federal documents.[13]

What's worse than losing your good name?

"The worst-case scenario is when the thief commits crimes in the victim's name," says Beth Givens, director of the Privacy Rights Clearinghouse. "We learned of a case where the imposter was a major drug dealer, using the identity of a high-tech company president. This man travels out of the country often and has to carry a letter from law enforcement which explains he is not the drug dealer, because he gets pulled into secondary inspection every time he comes back to the U.S. Recently law enforcement from another state, who had not read the entry on the FBI's NCIC crime data base completely, entered his bedroom in the early morning hours and tried to arrest him at gunpoint. He was able to convince them they were seeking the wrong person.

"Another case that came to our hotline involved an Hispanic man, a U.S. citizen, who was visiting relatives in Tijuana,

Mexico, across the border from San Diego. He was taken into secondary inspection by U.S. Customs on his return trip to San Diego. A search of his SSN showed he was wanted for a crime in the Bay Area. He was transported from San Diego to San Francisco and put in jail. It took him 10 days before one of the officers believed him, took his fingerprints as he had requested all along, and realized they had the wrong person."[14]

Death is certainly worse

Because identity theft is now often part and parcel of a slew of other crimes and, as we've seen, terrorist attacks, the stakes have risen immeasurably. Involvement, even peripherally, can be deadly.

In March 2002, FBI agents arrested L.C., a Tennessee motor vehicle license clerk, on charges that she helped five Middle Eastern men from New York obtain fraudulent Tennessee drivers' licenses.

The day before her scheduled court appearance, a Highway Patrolman discovered the woman's charred remains in a burning car a few miles from her Memphis home. The car—registered to one of the men arrested in the plot—had run off the highway and eventually hit a telephone pole.[15]

Federal investigators declared that the fire was set. "Her death was not the result of the crash itself," said Tennessee Highway Patrol Captain Jimmy Erwin. "Her death was by other means."[16]

Traces of gasoline on pieces of clothing retrieved from the vehicle certainly supported that conclusion, along with eyewitness accounts that she didn't try "to stop her car or take any evasive action…There was plenty of time for even an 'inattentive' driver [to avoid hitting the pole]."[17]

A state driver's license is one of the most effective documents an identity thief could have. With it, he or she can easily get a variety of other documents to create a broader identity.

Given that fact, one would assume the states have taken great pains to ensure the security of their licensing systems. If you did, you would be wrong. The arrest of 36 people in New Jersey in June 2002 showed just how easy it can be to get that important document.

In a well-organized conspiracy, "28 alleged brokers charged $1,200 to $2,000 for a state photo driver's license. People recruited to take driving tests and other exams received $250, while Division of Motor Vehicle clerks averaged $50 to $2,000 for each document they produced." Almost a quarter of those arrested had previously worked for the Division of Motor Vehicles.[18]

But an enterprising identity thief—or terrorist—needn't pay so much or deal with an organized ring. Mohamed Atta, the pilot of the first plane to hit the Twin Towers, got a Florida driver's license just by showing his Egyptian license. And two of the other hijackers, Hanji Hanjour and Khalid Almihbar, got Virginia drivers' licenses after simply paying someone $100 to swear they were residents of that state.

What about L.C. and the five New Yorkers? Why did they drive all the way to Tennessee in the first place?

Because Tennessee had stopped requiring aliens to produce proof that they were in the country legally.

It's a global problem

The problem of low-paid clerks selling identity thieves official documents certainly isn't confined to Tennessee or New Jersey...or to any of the states, for that matter.

A State Department probe revealed a way terrorists—or anyone attempting to enter the country illegally—can get the help of the United States government to do so. In July 2002, federal investigators arrested 31 Middle Easterners suspected of entering the U.S. by bribing American Embassy officials in Qatar for visas. According to a U.S. official, two of the 31 previously lived with the 9/11 terrorists.[19]

In June 2002, police discovered a program installed on student computers at universities in Florida, Arizona, Texas, and California that gave remote access to the students' credit card numbers, passwords, and e-mail. The program secretly made a record of everything typed on the computers, allowing a hacker to retrieve, at his or her leisure, any information entered into the system. Authorities were even more worried when they discovered that the program linked the college computers to a computer in Russia.[20]

Russia? One of the most dangerous identity thieves in the world—or more than one—is operating from there right now.

"For over a year," according to Bob Sullivan at MSNBC, "[a man who goes by the name of] Zilterio has been hacking into online companies and financial institutions, stealing data, then demanding extortion payments. Nine firms have paid him $150,000 quiet money, he claims...[though] there's no proof anyone has paid.

"'I hate to inform you that your account has been hacked.' Tens of thousands of Internet users have received a note beginning like that from Zilterio, whose real identity is a mystery. It's followed by personal details, such as name, address, e-mail address and credit card numbers...

"Zilterio, he claimed, is actually a group of eight hackers—three in Moscow, and five elsewhere in Russia...And extortion is just their hobby. The group spends most of its time engaging in other computer crimes, like auction fraud, credit card fraud, direct bank hacking..."[21]

The Nigerian Express

And Russia is certainly not the only country involved in this global information exchange. "The Nigerian Express," a complex association of Nigerian men and women involved in a variety of crimes, was busted in July of 2000.

They were involved in three distinct, but related, operations: distributing heroin in and around Queens County, New York; filing false or forged tax instruments; and massive identity theft and credit card fraud.

V.S., aka "Prince," was the leader of the Nigerian Express. He oversaw each of the three criminal operations through a separate director. According to a 268-count indictment, Prince and his cohorts stole over $1.4 million from 20 banks and credit card institutions in Maryland, Delaware, Illinois, New York, and Colorado.

Identifying victims and obtaining their personal information was relatively straightforward—they simply purchased copies of rental car agreements from a former employee of a car rental agency in Rhode Island for $20 each. Armed with names, addresses, Social Security numbers, credit card account numbers and copies of drivers licenses, they transferred balances from the unsuspecting victims' bank accounts into newly opened accounts under still other victims' names. The money was withdrawn almost as fast as it could be transferred. In some instances, they simply made direct cash withdrawals from victims' accounts or used stolen or forged convenience checks written from them.

"Our investigation," said Queens District Attorney Richard A. Brown, "revealed that [this group] had accumulated financial and personal information, including mothers' maiden names, of approximately 1,300 legitimate citizens from across the country, which gave the defendants access to about $10 million in credit."

"In addition," said the District Attorney, "[an accountant working with the group helped them] create forged Social Security cards, checks, driver's licenses, and State Department immigration visa applications in order to supply [them] with identification to open fraudulent bank accounts; allow aliens living in the New York area to file multiple copies of immigration lottery applications; and furnish illegal aliens with the documentation necessary to obtain employment."

What made cracking the gang particularly difficult was their inventive use of their native language to establish a seemingly unbreakable code, much like the famous Navajo "code-talkers" of World War II.

"[The district attorney's office] spent a year listening to wiretaps and scouring bank records. The phone conversations were not only in Yoruba, a Nigerian tribal language, but were also in code…[M]embers of the ring would refer, for instance, to the 'house of dance,' meaning 'disco,' which was the code for the Discover card. 'To do a Nigerian wiretap, you're in for a wild ride,' [noted bureau chief Diane] Peress."[22]

High technology yields high profits

Technology is making forgery easier than ever. K.D. and S.F. stole mail from residences and corner drop boxes in the San Francisco Bay Area. Using the personal information they obtained from the stolen mail, they created fake documents using high-end scanners and color printers. During a two-year period, the pair used phony ID's to steal more than $5 million.

The technology was also their undoing. Investigators determined that ink cartridges for their specialized color printer were available at only three local stores. When one of the suspects next made a purchase, police followed him to his residence.

Detectives found thousands of dollars worth of computers, digital cameras, scanners, printers, and hologram-imprinting devices, plus boxes of check stock and blank credit cards.[23]

The Secret Service recently busted two people caught with the identifiers (names, dates of birth, and Social Security numbers) of approximately 3,000 victims. These stolen identifiers were used to open numerous fraudulent bank accounts, ATM and credit cards, and cellular telephone service in the names of the victims.

When they were arrested, the evidence seized included sophisticated computer equipment that was being used to manufacture false INS I-551 cards ("green cards") and other identification documents. Also seized were numerous checkbooks, bank statements, financial records, cell phones, and credit cards, all registered in names of other individuals, and two "point of sale terminals"—used to read credit card magnetic stripes.

If you can't beat 'em, join 'em

It's always been easier to break into a bank, jewelry store, or armored car with the help of someone "inside." Why work to disarm an alarm system when your cohort can just switch it off for you?

Identity thieves have also discovered it never hurts to have a friend "on the inside." As *Bottom Line Personal* recently reported, "Organized crime members apply for bank-teller jobs or pay other tellers to forge savings account withdrawals and steal money.

"The stolen information is then keyed into the bank's operating system. This way, it appears that the customer actually visited a teller's window. By keeping withdrawal amounts low, the scam goes undetected until the victim receives his/her monthly statement."[24]

One man stole the identities of more than 100 people by hooking up with a woman who had worked in the payroll department of a cellular telephone company. Using the confidential employee information she supplied, the man was able to access the victims' online brokerage accounts and transfer money to his own accounts. One victim alone lost $287,000.[25]

A California man stockpiled the private bank account information of an insurance company's policyholders while temporarily employed there. After his short stint of real work, he used that information to deposit more than 4,000 counterfeit bank drafts for nearly $1 million into his own accounts.[26]

Federal prosecutors in Brooklyn, New York, recently indicted a former employee of a major insurance company who stole a database containing 60,000 names and Social Security numbers and posted them for sale on a variety of electronic bulletin boards.[27]

Also in New York, a woman employed in a clerical position at the New York State Insurance Fund stole the personal identifying information of thousands of state employees and citizens who dealt with the fund. While still at work, she used her computer to obtain credit and goods—using the names of other individuals, including fellow employees. She also provided personal data to accomplices who used the information to steal even more merchandise and services.

When she was arrested, investigators discovered not only thousands of records from the State Insurance Fund, but many more from the college at which she had previously worked.[28]

Baby, you can drive my car

While insurance companies look like an identity thief's dream, an enterprising imposter can find information just about anywhere. E.R. a former manager of a Detroit car rental agency, stole hundreds of completed rental applications, each one containing the name, address, telephone number, date of birth, Social Security number, driver license number, and credit account number of the customer applying to rent a vehicle. He reportedly traded them to the owner of an escort service, who provided him with the free, uh, services of his, er, employees. Needless to say, the escort agency owner used the stolen identity information to access the victims' credit accounts.[29] Someone should have told "Prince" and his fellow Nigerians they didn't have to actually *pay* for car rental applications.

But why make just customers into victims. Aren't your fellow employees worthy?

P.W. was employed as an information source supervisor at a Detroit car dealership. He simply used his fellow employees' names and identifying information (right there in the files) to obtain a series of American Express corporate cards. He then purchased electronics, clothing, jewelry, camera equipment and enjoyed the finest hotels and restaurants in New York City, Tennessee, Kentucky, and elsewhere.

The truly adventurous imposter does not limit him- or herself to a single theft or method.

In a recent case in Oregon, a ring of thieves obtained identity information by stealing mail, garbage, and recycling material, by breaking into cars, and by hacking into Websites and personal computers. They stole pre-approved credit card solicitations, activated the cards, and had them sent to drop boxes or third-party addresses.

Another scam involved taking names, dates of birth, and SSNs from discarded medical, insurance, or tax forms and obtaining credit cards at various sites on the Internet.

Before they were arrested, they had gained access to 400 credit card accounts and rung up $400,000 in purchases.

In Denver, Colorado, another group—the largest identity-theft ring in state history—was equally enterprising. The group's methods ranged from sophisticated counterfeiting to scavenger hunts in dumpsters. Forty-eight suspects were accused of cashing at least 790 fraudulent checks for nearly half a million dollars. They also paid people for copies of company paychecks, which the group would then use to glean information and create more counterfeit checks.[30]

Whom can you trust?

Despite the prevalence of fraud, we can take solace that there are at least some individuals we can trust—surely doctors, teachers, preachers, and the police are our bulwark against the rising tide of identity theft.

Aren't they?

An ex-con, fresh out of prison, went dumpster diving and found a wallet containing a California driver's license and Social Security card. With the help of an accomplice, he opened 20 credit accounts at major department stores, banks, and cell phone companies. Without changing the victim's address, they ran up bills for several months until the victim began receiving bills that didn't belong to him, called the credit bureaus and had a fraud alert added to his reports.

The ex-con was busted when he tried to return merchandise previously purchased on a bogus credit account.

It all would have ended there, a minor footnote in our story, except that the now fearful con told police about a larger operation run by a couple of San Bernardino physicians. When they investigated, police discovered that the doctors had already stolen the identity of another victim, using it to apply for a $60,000 loan for a Mercedes. When local banks were contacted, they found several credit applications using the same addresses and phone numbers for residences and employers, all under the doctors' new identities.

Police pounced. The raid uncovered numerous IDs, including those belonging to two individuals who were in prison at the time.

The doctors were eventually indicted on dozens of counts of identity theft and fraud.[31]

Well, maybe we can't rely on doctors.

A woman who assumed the identities of at least three people, including a teacher, was recently sentenced to four years in prison (on top of the five she got for a previous fraud case) and 16 years probation. R.D. was arrested in May 2001, in her fourth-grade classroom.

The probationary period was apt, since the U.S. Postal Service was able to show that R.D. had been using three different

49

aliases for the past 20 years. She was finally caught when one of her victims tried to purchase a home but couldn't because of the loans and purchases that had been made in her name by R.D.

Two down, two to go.

According to the *Memphis Commercial Appeal*, the pastor of the local Baptist church "used the name and Social Security number of a woman who attended the church to open a cell phone account. He later sold the phone, still in her name, to someone else."

Church authorities had no warning that the preacher was a faker...unless you count the thousands of dollars of other merchandise he bought using church funds. Or the $25,000 he owed in child support.[32]

The *Commercial Appeal* also recently reported that "one of the 24 people indicted this week in an identity theft scheme targeting Federal Housing Authority mortgage loans and city down payment assistance loans" was a local police officer.[33]

Which makes it only fitting for Memphis to be the site of our final embarrassment. The head of the largest identity theft ring ever prosecuted in federal court in Memphis had two businesses: installing home alarm systems and helping people repair their bad credit!

"In this case, the victims had no way of ascertaining that anything was out of the ordinary," the judge said. "I can't think of anything that surpasses it that I've seen." "It" involved more than $2 million in financing for 38 vehicles and eight houses during 2000.

"[The judge] estimated [the imposter] made at least 1,000 attempts at creating fraudulent identities."[34]

I think trust just took a dive.

I know who I am, but who are you?

Even thieves can get confused about who they really are.

In December 2001, E.F. and L.F. were arrested in a Riverside, California, parking lot…in a stolen truck filled with more than a thousand pieces of mail and dozens of personal checks. E.F. copped a plea for auto theft and went to prison for a couple of years.[35]

L.F., on the other hand, tried to push her luck…as well as a new identity. In April 2002, she opened an account at the local credit union using the ID of a woman whose purse was stolen a month earlier. She was arrested trying to cash a forged check when an alert teller saw that it had been altered.

Before police could determine who she really was, L.F. posted bail, using her false identity, of course. Police probably figured she was gone for good when she failed to make her court date. But two weeks later, she was stopped while driving a stolen car. She gave the officer yet another fake name…and the ID to match. This time, however, the officer recognized her from her previous booking photo.[36]

We're the government. We're on your side.

Even entire agencies can have their "identities" stolen.

One enterprising group posed as FTC reps and called people to "confirm" their inclusion on a Federally maintained list of consumers who did not want to receive telemarketing calls. While "confirming" their participation, of course, the imposters managed to extract Social Security, bank account, and credit card numbers from some of the less-sophisticated victims.

In a series of press releases and on the government's Identity Theft Website (*www.consumer/gov/idtheft*), the FTC took pains to clarify that once you sign up with a state's "do not call" registry, there is no need to "confirm" anything, especially personal information. And that a *Federal* "do not call" registry doesn't even exist.[37]

So, a new thief found another way to impersonate the same agency. In June 2002, an FTC investigation into a bogus work-at-home scheme became a bit more complicated after a man pretending to be an FTC employee e-mailed hundreds of the scam's victims seeking personal information to be used as "evidence" in the investigation.

And in May 2002, the Internal Revenue Service warned consumers about a multi-state scam. Thousands of people received phony IRS letters that told them to fill out and fax in an IRS form (helpfully enclosed) within seven days or the government would withhold 31 percent of the interest on their bank accounts. The form asked for account numbers, PIN codes, passwords, date of birth, mother's maiden name, and other highly personal information. Victims from Maine to California, New York to Texas, and Georgia to Washington fell for the scam and supplied the information—with dire results.

Three different forms were used as part of the scam. One phony form—W-8888—bore no relation to any existing IRS form. It merely asked for a plethora of personal data.

The second, according to the IRS, was "labeled 'W-9095, Application Form for Certificate Status/Ownership for Withholding Tax.' [It] appears to [have been] an attempt to mimic the genuine IRS Form W-9, 'Request for Taxpayer Identification Number and Certification.'"

Another form made no attempt to mimic anything. It was titled Form W-8BEN "Certificate of Foreign Status of Beneficial Owner for United States Tax Withholding." Well, there *is* a legitimate Form W-8BEN, but *it* doesn't request the personal information that the phony one did.[38]

Clearly, the identity thieves are a creative bunch. But they couldn't succeed—heck, they couldn't even *exist*—if not for their partners in crime. We'll expose them in the next chapter.

Chapter

Partners in Crime

Identity thieves could not be successful without the help of numerous "partners in crime," who furnish them with their victims' personal information, give them the means to use such stolen information, or both.

There's certainly enough blame to go around. Credit card companies, banks, the credit reporting agencies, commercial mail receiving agencies, Internet brokers, the Federal government, states and localities, and law enforcement can all claim a share. They have all made it distressingly easy for an identity thief to get *and use* someone else's personal information.

The credit reporting agencies

CRAs such as Equifax, Experian, and Transunion profit by selling your personal data to credit grantors, employers, landlords, and others. They are undoubtedly the identity thieves' most valuable partners in crime. Without access to CRA files, opportunities for identity theft would be severely limited.[1]

CRAs are the largest private distributors of detailed personal information in the country. Practically every American adult is listed in the CRA files. In addition to basic identifying information ("header data"), such as your name, Social Security number, employer(s), address(es), and telephone number(s), the CRA databases include information on your credit accounts, payment history, public record items (bankruptcy, judgments, tax liens, foreclosures, etc.) and recent inquiries.

"Of course," notes the Privacy Rights Clearinghouse, "there are supposed to be ways to protect that data. When a 'fraud alert' is placed on a victim's credit file, for example, the credit bureau reports to credit issuers that the subject of the report is a victim of fraud. The creditor is supposed to contact the victim at the phone number provided in the fraud alert in order to determine if it is an imposter or the rightful individual applying for credit. Obviously, if the credit bureau does not adequately report the presence of an alert (which often happens when only a credit score is reported), or if the credit grantor fails to detect the fraud alert (which is a common experience of victims), the imposter is able to obtain additional lines of credit in the victim's name."[2]

The number of seven-year fraud alerts placed on consumer credit files is considered by many consumer reporting agency officials to be the most reliable measure of identity theft. One of the three major consumer reporting agencies estimated that its seven-year fraud alerts increased 36 percent in just one year—from 65,600 in 1999 to 89,000 in 2000. A second agency reported that its alerts increased 53 percent in two years.[3]

A survey jointly undertaken by the Privacy Rights Clearinghouse and California Public Interest Research Group (CALPIRG) revealed how effective the CRAs' efforts to protect consumers have been: "Victims reported that all of the credit bureaus were difficult to reach, but the hardest one to get in touch with, and the one about which most negative comments were made, was Equifax. Over one-third of the respondents reported not being able to speak with a 'live' representative at Equifax or Experian despite numerous attempts. Less than two-thirds felt that the credit bureaus had been effective in removing the fraudulent accounts or placing a fraud alert on their reports. Despite the placement of a fraud alert on a victim's credit report, almost half (46 percent) of the respondents' financial fraud recurred on each credit report."[4]

When CRA files are compromised, the danger can be extensive. In May 2002, thieves posing as Ford Motor Credit personnel—possibly using company passwords—gained access to a database used by Experian and downloaded the personal information of 13,000 customers. "The credit files included Social Security numbers, addresses, account numbers, creditor names and payment history—everything needed to commit credit fraud."[5]

The credit card companies

The hunger of the credit card companies for even more people charging more things is costing them a fortune, as identity thieves take advantage of their procedures. As explained in the Chapter 3, pre-approved credit offers are an identity thief's delight. Well, in 1998, the companies mailed out 3.4 *billion* such offers.

In an Oregon case, which involved 400 credit card accounts and $400,000 in bogus bills, "the thieves found most credit card companies to be unwilling allies. One of the thieves boasted about successfully persuading [one bank] to grant a higher credit limit on a fraudulently obtained credit card account."[6]

Commercial Mail Receiving Agencies[7]

Since 1996, the Queens County (NY) District Attorney's Office has dismantled four multi-million dollar financial fraud enterprises who owed their very existence and survival to Commercial Mail Receiving Agencies. (The most notorious, dubbed the "Nigerian Express," was discussed in the Chapter 3-*Ed.*)

"Operation Silver Parrot," for example, was an eight-month investigation that resulted in a 200-count indictment against eight Nigerians.

This ring would obtain personal information about a potential victim from any number of available sources and then "become the victim." Once a victim was identified, his or her mail would be diverted to a "temporary" address—one of hundreds of Commercial Mail Receiving Agencies (CMRA) that were rented by the criminals in the names of the victims. Within a 30-day period, by looking at the victim's mail, an entire financial profile could be constructed, after which the ring systematically drained all available credit and cash accounts, even to the point of using the victim's frequent flier miles.

(Since that investigation, the United States Postal Service has tightened its controls on "change of address forms." A "move verification letter" is now sent to the original address, warning potential victims that they may have been targeted by an identity theft ring.)

The leader, Olishina Adecombie, told prosecutors that he had personally made $8 million which he had prudently invested in apartment buildings in his native country. When he was arrested, investigators found papers for a new Mercedes-Benz that had been shipped to Nigeria. When officials asked him about it, Adecombie asked what color the car was...so he could figure out *which* Mercedes they were talking about. (It was gold.) The last known address on the New York motor vehicle registration was a Commercial Mail Receiving Agency.

Following the adage "if you can't beat 'em, join 'em," the district attorney's office set up their own Commercial Mail Receiving Agency with thoughts of Kevin Costner's line in *Field of Dreams*, "if you build it, they will come." Well, they came in such overwhelming numbers that prosecutors were forced to concentrate on only one of the many rings that started operating out of their bogus CMRA.

As a result of obtaining court-ordered wiretaps, investigators were able to literally hear the ring in operation. Members of the ring would call credit reporting agencies posing as consumers seeking copies of credit reports to be sent to their "new addresses." Once the ring had a specific credit report, they would systematically contact each creditor, notifying them of the "new address and apartment number," and request that replacement credit cards or checks be sent to the "new address." It would, of course, be a mailbox at the bogus Commercial Mail Receiving Agency.

One particularly interesting conversation was a call to a major credit card issuer in which the imposter claimed to be on vacation, staying at the "Hotel Kennedy." He indicated he had lost his credit card and needed a new one mailed to him at the hotel, where he was staying in room 142. The address he gave was, of course, the CMRA. Within two days, a new card arrived at the location—via Federal Express—addressed to "Hotel Kennedy, room 142." This example is not an exception to the rule. During the course of the investigation, thousands of dollars worth of merchandise from mail order catalogs and Internet sites was delivered in the same manner.

"Operation Black Leather" was a multi-million dollar merchant fraud enterprise operating in New York, New Jersey, California and Florida. The thieves set up fake stores that purported to sell leather apparel (hence the term "Black Leather"). Each business opened merchant processor accounts with banks all over the country.

A merchant processor account processes credit card transactions for a business, requests payment from the issuer, and deposits the money in the merchant's bank account...in one day. In Black Leather, the con artists opened accounts with anywhere from three to 10 merchant processors, stole account information from consumers at gas stations, restaurants, and retail stores, then charged their accounts for purchases of leather goods from the bogus stores. As soon as the money was placed in the defendants' accounts, it was withdrawn.

After a couple of weeks, the thieves would close up one business and open up another under a different name somewhere else. They were finally busted when a Dominican nun noticed that she was charged for the purchase of a leather coat from a Queens, N. Y. store. The good sister was a very credible witness when she testified that she had never worn a leather coat, much less bought one.

These imposters used CMRAs for all aspects of their operations. When they incorporated the fake businesses, the corporate address was a CMRA. When they applied for a merchant processor account, the address was a CMRA. All the bank documents led to CMRAs. The defendants sent materials to co-conspirators in other states at CMRA addresses. Two of the fake storefronts actually had no address at all, and were merely mailboxes at CMRAs. (The financial institutions were supplied with Polaroids of a nonexistent store, complete with temporary sign.) Of course, all of the CMRA mailboxes were rented with phony identifications, so that when the defendants "busted out" of a storefront, all leads led to an abandoned mailbox under someone else's name at a Commercial Mail Receiving Agency.

The Internet

At a September 13, 2000 appearance before the House Committee on Banking and Financial Services, an FTC official testified, in part:

"The Internet has dramatically altered the potential occurrence and impact of identity theft. First, the Internet provides access to identifying information through both illicit and legal means. The global publication of identifying details that previously were available only to a select few increases the potential for misuse of that information.

Second, the ability of the identity thief to purchase goods and services from innumerable e-merchants expands the potential harm to the victim through numerous purchases. The explosion of financial services offered online, such as mortgages, credit cards, bank accounts, and loans, provides a sense of anonymity to those potential identity thieves who would not risk committing identity theft in a face-to-face transaction."

In another hearing, a Department of Justice official declared: "Internet fraud, in all of its forms, is one of the fastest growing and most pervasive forms of white-collar crime... Regrettably, criminal exploitation of the Internet now encompasses a wide variety of securities and other investment schemes, online auction schemes, credit-card fraud, financial institution fraud, and identity theft.

"A January 2001 study by Meridien Research...reports that with the continuing growth of e-commerce, payment card fraud on the Internet will increase worldwide from $1.6 billion in 2000 to $15.5 billion by 2005...Foreign law enforcement authorities also regard Internet fraud as a growing problem. Earlier this year, the European Commission reported that in 2000, payment card fraud in the European Union increased by 50 percent to $553 million in fraudulent transactions, and noted that fraud was increasing most in relation to remote payment transactions, especially on the Internet. Similarly, the International Chamber of Commerce's Commercial Crime Service reported that nearly two-thirds of all cases it handled in 2000 involved online fraud."[8]

Local and state government authorities

Local and state government authorities get their share of the blame. Numerous Departments of Motor Vehicles (DMVs) sell their lists of registered drivers and car owners. For a fee, many will conduct customized searches of driver's license and car registration records.

Criminals can obtain unlisted telephone numbers, Social Security numbers, physical description (height, weight, etc.), and more simply by sifting through property deeds and court case data, generally available for a small fee at the local court house, tax assessor's office, or county clerk's office. This information is also made available to brokers who, in turn, sell it to potential identity thieves too lazy to walk to the courthouse.

While most of this information has always been in the public record, access to it was limited to people able to wind their way through complicated county court indices. Now that this information can be found on the Internet, it's just a keystroke away.

Many identity thieves don't strike just once—they victimize hundreds of victims in many states, even many countries. This makes for a jurisdictional nightmare, especially in the U.S. where 9/11, among other examples, exposed the glaring communication problems between law enforcement entities, especially when local, state, and national agencies are involved simultaneously.

Until *all* of these entities—the credit card companies and other financial institutions, credit reporting agencies, commercial mail receiving agencies, and government at all levels—band together to attack identity theft with all the tools at their command, the stories of victims, like those in Chapter 5, will continue to occur with frightening regularity.

Chapter

5

Who Are the Victims?

Do you think you're not a target because you're not a rich and famous celebrity, business tycoon, or professional? While identity thieves would certainly prefer victims with a "platinum" variety of juicy credit card and bank accounts to plunder, some will settle for anyone—dead or alive, rich or poor, young or old. Just as long as they have a name.

We have been talking so far about a crime called "identity theft", but we really need to differentiate between two completely different kinds of identity theft: "**Application fraud** or **account takeover fraud** occurs when the imposter uses a victim's existing credit accounts. **True name fraud** is when the imposter opens new credit accounts in the name of the victim."[1]

Whichever occurs, the true loss is rarely financial. "Victims are not liable for the bills accumulated by the imposters, thanks to federal law. But they do have the anxiety and frustration of spending months, even years, regaining their financial health and restoring their good credit history."[2]

Most of you are probably already in shock. You may have heard tales of identity theft, perhaps when the stories of 9/11 came out. But it shouldn't really have come as such a shock. We should have been warned. Both Broadway and Hollywood have featured plays and movies based on identity theft.

In "Six Degrees of Separation," an ID thief purports to be Sidney Poitier's son and lives a luxurious life while trading on his famous "father's" name.

And just recently, Matt Damon plotted to take over the identity of Jude Law (and the affections of Gwyneth Paltrow, a not inconsequential "extra") in "The Talented Mr. Ripley."

But these were, of course, fiction. Nothing like that happens in the real world, certainly not to celebrities like Poitier or Damon or Paltrow.

But it did to Tiger, Jerry, and (almost) Michael.

Keep your eye on the ball, Tiger

"Tiger Woods says he never rented a moving truck in Sacramento. He says he never put $100 down on a used luxury car. And golf's best player says he never gave [F.M.] of Sacramento permission to charge $17,000 on his credit cards.

"...[F.M.] used Woods' real name—Eldrick T. Woods—and [his] Social Security number to obtain a fake drivers license [and] apply for credit cards in Woods' name...A...storage locker rented in Woods' name was found stuffed with TVs, videocassette recorders, furniture and other items. Woods denies renting the locker or purchasing the items found inside."[3]

An almost magic impersonation

Claiming to be Los Angeles Lakers' team owner Jerry Buss's son, Jerry Jr., a man tried opening a brokerage account with a $161,171.32 state tax refund check payable to Buss that had been stolen from the mail. His accomplice opened a second account with the brokerage firm to convince employees the funds from the check were being invested in an energy company.

An alert employee knew that Buss did not have a son named Jerry and called the FBI.

The men were arrested and charged with possession of stolen mail, conspiracy, and identity theft. Authorities said one of the men tried to use money from a previous scam to post bail. That scam had involved using checks stolen from a trust set up by former "My Three Sons" star Fred MacMurray and his wife, actress June Haver.

Michael Jordan actually avoided problems—this time—because the man trying to steal his identity thought it necessary to find someone to actually impersonate Jordan (or, at least, his wife Juanita). Caught before he could do so, the thief *did* already have the number of one of Jordan's bank accounts. Guess he wasn't content to "be *like* Mike"; he wanted to *be* Mike.[4]

Maybe a little too friendly

Some of us are just ripe for the picking. Being nice can be a problem if an imposter is ready and willing to take advantage. One of C.T.'s friends asked if she could transfer her house into C.T.'s name because she had some "tax problems." In addition to agreeing to help her friend, C.T. also co-signed a mortgage note on her friend's house. After falling behind on the mortgage payments, the friend filed for bankruptcy...in C.T.'s name. The friend surprisingly made payments on "C.T.'s" bankruptcy plan for several *years!* C.T. didn't even find out about the bankruptcy until she applied for a vacation loan, which was denied because of the bankruptcy filing and the large home loan (her friend's, not hers) listed on her credit record.[5]

At the request of her landlord, 18-year-old Y.Q. signed some documents he said he needed to "help him own property." Y.Q. didn't realize that the documents named *her* as a co-owner of an apartment building guaranteed by a Federal Housing Administration loan. Some time later, she was denied credit because of the two bankruptcy filings listed on her credit record. Only then did she discover that her landlord had filed for bankruptcy in her name to stay foreclosure on one of his rental properties.

In fact, he had filed *multiple* bankruptcy cases in the names of *numerous* current or former tenants and employees.[6]

You're never too young

K.C. received an official-looking letter addressed to her son Ryan. She opened the letter and discovered that it directed Ryan to appear at a meeting of creditors convened as part of his bankruptcy case. K.C. was shocked because she knew Ryan had never filed for bankruptcy.

Ryan was five years old.

K.C. suspected that Ryan's father—her estranged husband—filed the case to stay an impending foreclosure of the family home. He had filed for bankruptcy twice before, and his second case had been dismissed less than three months earlier.[7]

The FBI is currently investigating a case in which Social Security numbers for children of various ages have been sold to individuals with bad credit for future use in obtaining credit. As part of the sale, the buyers formed companies which they used to falsely report positive credit information on these SSNs to the credit reporting agencies, including bogus loan payoffs and information on other fictitious credit accounts that were supposedly paid off. This positive information boosted the user's credit history and, thereby, his or her credit score.

Next the users applied to legitimate credit issuers, including mortgage companies, and obtained credit in their own names due to their now positive credit reports. Since the victims are children who won't be applying for any credit anytime soon, they are not aware their Social Security numbers have already been stolen. So in the meantime, they're not filing any complaints with law enforcement, the credit reporting agencies or any of the defrauded creditors. When they later become old enough to try to establish credit, they will learn they already *have* a credit history. And it *isn't* a good one.[8]

You're never too "smart"

As recently reported in *National Jurist* magazine, "at least 10 students at Yeshiva University's Benjamin N. Cardozo School of Law in New York say they are victims of credit card fraud, and the school has opened an investigation for possible campus links."

One of the victims was R.G.: "I found out about it because I tried to move apartments and sign a new lease. It came back that my credit was horrible. Somebody had taken out two credit cards, and they changed the address to Brooklyn. They ran up big bills and then never paid them."

Officials speculated that the thieves had intercepted a mass mailing of pre-approved credit card offers. As Brian Rauer, vice president and general counsel of the Better Business Bureau's Metro New York chapter warned, "A lot of people don't realize that if you throw [them] away, someone can pick [them] up and send them in."[9]

You're never too old

Four Detroit-area men and one woman worked together to locate houses that were owned free and clear by elderly people. They would then steal the identities of the true owners and strip the equity out of the houses. How? They used two different methods.

In the first, they faked a "re-financing" of the property—withdrawing equity, obtaining a mortgage in the true owner's name, then defaulting on it.

Alternatively, they would fake a "straw sale" of the home. This involved forging a quit claim from the true owner to one of the imposters, who would in turn, "sell" the home to one of the other imposters. The latter would mortgage the property. The mortgage company would give the proceeds to the first imposter. The second imposter would simply default on the mortgage and walk away.

In either case, the elderly couple or person wouldn't have a clue that their house had literally been sold right out from under them.[10]

You don't even have to be alive

When the IRS rejected the tax return of Jim and Karen T., they couldn't figure out why...until they were told that someone else had claimed their son, Eric, as a dependent to get a $1,500 tax credit. Their *dead* son, Eric. "[Jim and Karen] believe the thief got [Eric]'s information from a genealogy Website, where he is still listed," reported CBSNEWS.com. "Ironically, they still don't know who [stole their son's identity], because the IRS protects the thief's identity[!]"[11]

You could know the law

C.R., a prominent California law professor, thought the letter at the bottom of her mailbox was just another unsolicited credit card offer and was about to throw it away. But when she opened it, she was surprised to see it was a notice confirming her change of residence to an address in Fresno, California. C.R. had never lived in Fresno. Nor did she ever *plan* to live in Fresno.

She immediately called the credit card company to notify them that they had made a mistake. The representative at the company insisted that *they* hadn't made a mistake at all—*she* had applied for a Visa card and listed her current address as a *previous* address, with a new address in Fresno. It took several minutes of arguing for C.R. to learn the issue date and other pertinent information about this bogus change of address request. She then contacted her local police department.

Police discovered the new address was merely a mail drop—a private mail receiving service. The manager of the mail drop provided the officers with copies of the driver's license and application used by the person renting the box. The license appeared authentic and had all of C.R.'s correct identifying information, except, of course, for that new address in Fresno.

Oh, and the photo of a middle-aged Caucasian woman.

C.R. was African American.

Investigators went to the address listed on the driver's license, where they arrested two women who had been recently released from prison on assorted fraud and theft charges. It turned out that the women had stolen the identities of more than two hundred prominent women listed in various "Who's Who" directories.

The identity thieves also gathered information freely and conveniently available from the university's catalog and Website, establishing accounts in the names of several prominent faculty members in addition to C.R.

The professors were targeted because of their relatively high pay, solid backgrounds, and stability. Other victims included doctors, attorneys, university presidents, and successful business executives.[12]

Be the head of a major company

The FBI's New York Bureau recently investigated a case that included the use of the personal identifying information of six prominent executives, three of whom were dead. Starting with just the names, the thief (later arrested) paid Internet information brokers to obtain the executives' Social Security numbers. Armed with the SSNs, it was relatively easy to get a list of bank accounts and credit card numbers for each.

At which point the impersonations began. At least the thief had good taste—authorities reported he purchased nearly a million dollars worth of diamonds and Rolex watches over the Internet, either wire-transferring money from one of his victim's bank accounts or using one of their credit card numbers.[13]

Three recently indicted thieves in Michigan only needed to steal a single identity, that of a retired K-mart executive, and make a single transaction to (almost) steal more than $200,000. All they had to do after accumulating the necessary personal information was sell his stock options—176,000 of them, at a price of $10 per share. Net profit? $212,234.73, deposited into a commercial brokerage account they had opened in the victim's name. They were caught when they presented a forged check to withdraw the funds.[14]

But being rich and a celebrity is best of all

Besides being rich and famous, what do billionaire investor Warren Buffett, Microsoft co-founder Paul Allen, Steven Spielberg, Ted Turner, Martha Stewart, George Lucas, Oprah Winfrey, Ross Perot, and New York City mayor Michael Bloomberg have in common?

Their identities were stolen by the same Manhattan busboy—a high school dropout, no less—in what authorities have called the largest Internet fraud in history.[15]

"When A.V. was arrested in March 2001, he had 800 fraudulent credit cards and 20,000 blank credit cards. Police said at the time he had ordered a type of machine that could emboss them...[A search of his home] revealed photographs, Social

Security numbers, dates of birth, and addresses of more than 200 CEOs and more than 400 credit card numbers with matching addresses and personal information."[16]

At least he thought big—when he was caught, he was in the process of trying to transfer more than *$80 million* from his victims' bank and brokerage accounts into fraudulently opened accounts.

At least bankers are safe...aren't they?

In 1999, the Chief Credit Officer of Household International, a leading provider of consumer financial services and credit card products in the United States, Canada, and the United Kingdom, testified before Congress. His perspective was twofold: From his professional experience at Household...and as a victim of identity theft. Excerpts of his testimony are downright chilling:

"Household takes the issue of identity theft very seriously... In 1998, Household had more than 18,000 incidences of true-name fraud, with claims in excess of $35 million... As an aside, it is not at all uncommon for a family member to commit identity theft upon another family member. In our experience at Household, we find that *50 percent of all incidences of identity theft are committed by another family member.*

"Several years ago, unbeknownst to me, someone obtained my personal information, including my Social Security number, and then proceeded to open several credit card and retail credit accounts in my name. The perpetrator had my address changed to a location in Philadelphia. For these accounts, I received no statements or other information about the accounts. After opening these fraudulent accounts, the perpetrator proceeded to incur debts of tens of thousands of dollars...

"...[E]ven though I have been in the consumer credit business for over 30 years, I intentionally worked through the entire process of trying to correct my personal situation myself; and I did not let anyone know in the credit reporting industry or even in the companies where I knew the senior executives that were carrying the balances on my accounts that this had happened...

"I was unaware of any of this activity until one day when my wife received a telephone call at home from a collection agency after the debts had been delinquent for 60 days. It was at this time that I realized the scope of the problem and began the lengthy and painstaking process of repairing my credit record. I spent countless hours dealing with credit grantors and credit bureaus sorting out this problem...

"While I was ultimately able to successfully resolve the situation after 18 months, I am nonetheless keenly aware of the problems related to identity theft and the difficulty in combating them. I believe it is fair to state that, in my experience, both the credit bureaus and creditors have become more sensitized and effective in dealing with this problem."[17]

Same time, next decade

Sometimes it takes much longer than 60 days to discover your name is no longer your own.

One victim's ID was stolen 10 years ago by a high school buddy who used it to open various bank accounts and credit cards. His record was destroyed and he spent the next several years rebuilding his credit rating.

Meanwhile, the perpetrator continued a life of petty crime and was arrested 10 years later for unrelated charges. After he got out of jail, he used his friend's newly restored ID *again* to start over with a new crime spree.[18]

In a similar case, the FTC related the story of one caller of its identity theft hotline who had reported his wallet stolen in 1992. He was unaware he had become a victim of identity theft until 1999, when he was arrested for a crime committed in 1993...by the identity thief. He spent several nights in jail before finally being allowed to post bail. Once he started investigating, he discovered "he" was wanted in several states on a wide variety of warrants. The FTC concluded that "this example, while unusual, is not unique."

Which should make all of us sleep a lot better tonight...

Why not just steal a company's identity?

A band of thieves in San Jose, California, decided that stealing a person's identity, even the identities of hundreds of people, was just too time-consuming and small-time. So they simply took over the corporate identities of some of Silicon Valley's biggest high-tech firms. By duplicating corporate logos and impersonating executives—brazenly using the actual names of officers and managers listed on corporate Websites and in annual reports—they found that a number of leasing companies were more than happy to lend them hundreds of thousands of dollars. The leasing companies were ecstatic that these big companies wanted to work with them.

Local detectives eventually tracked the two men behind the scheme, who were operating out of a motor home in a trailer park. When they were arrested, police found 15 more fraudulent loan packages already prepared.[19]

Chapter

How to Reduce Your Risk

Notice I did not entitle this chapter, "How to *Eliminate* Your Risk."

I couldn't. Just as I can't promise that implementing every suggestion on the following pages will guarantee that you won't be victimized by an imposter.

You are still vulnerable.

We all are.

But like the mugger who would (understandably) prefer to prey on the little old lady with the big handbag rather than the imposing young man with the bulging biceps, any precautions you take to make an identity thief's "job" tougher may just convince him or her to seek a less troublesome victim.

So what can you do to at least minimize the risk you face? The Department of Justice has suggested that you just remember the word **SCAM**:[1]

S Be *stingy* about giving out your personal information to others unless you have a reason to trust them, whether you're at home, on the telephone, online, out and about, or on an extended vacation or business trip.

At home

Even if you've never served in the military, you can adapt one of their catch phrases: Put your personal information on a "need-to-know" basis. Your credit card company may need to know your mother's maiden name to verify you are who you say you are when you call to inquire about your account. But someone who calls you and says he's from your bank *does not* need to know that information—it's already on file at the bank. Barring a bank or financial institution so insensitive to the identity theft problem that it would actually seek to "confirm" such sensitive data on the telephone, the *only* purpose of such a call is to steal that information.

Put passwords on your credit card, bank, and phone accounts. Memorize them, change them regularly, and don't share them, even with family or friends. Avoid using your mother's maiden name, date of birth, the last four digits of your Social Security number, or your phone number—an identity thief may already have stolen them. If so, you have just given him or her access to your money.

Do not give out personal information on the phone, through the mail, or over the Internet unless you have initiated the contact or know with whom you're dealing. Identity thieves may pose as representatives of banks, Internet service providers, even government agencies to get you to reveal your SSN, mother's maiden name, financial account numbers, and other identifying information. Legitimate organizations with whom you do business already have the information they need and should not have to ask you for it.

If someone you don't know calls you on the telephone and offers you the chance to receive a new credit card, "fabulous" prize, or other valuable item, *but* asks for personal information, be sure to request a written application form. If they won't give one to you, tell them you're not interested and hang up. If they will, review the application carefully when you receive it and make sure it's from a company or financial institution that's well-known and reputable. The Better Business Bureau can give you information about businesses you want to avoid

Give out your SSN only when absolutely necessary. Ask to use other types of identifiers when possible.

Your employer and financial institution will likely need your SSN for wage and tax reporting purposes. Other private businesses may ask you for your SSN to do a credit check, such as when you apply for a car loan. You don't *have* to give a business your SSN just because they ask for it. If someone asks for your SSN, *you* should ask the following questions:

♦ Why do you need my SSN?

♦ How will my SSN be used?

♦ What law requires me to give you my SSN?

♦ What will happen if I don't give you my SSN?

A business may claim that unless you provide them with your SSN, they won't deliver the product or service you want. While this may be a factor in your deciding to give them that information, the decision is still yours. And it *can* be, "No thanks."

Before you reveal *any* identifying information, find out how it will be used and whether it will be shared with others. Ask if you have a choice about the use of your information. If so, can you choose to have it kept confidential?

The more information that you have printed on your personal checks—such as your Social Security number or home telephone number—the more personal data you are routinely giving to people who don't "need to know" that information.

Keep items with personal information in a safe place, and be cautious about where you store them in your home, especially if you have roommates, employ outside help, or have frequent visitors. Consider purchasing a home safe for your most important records or renting a safe deposit box at your local bank.

Keep the three items identity thieves most covet—your Social Security card, birth certificate, and passport—in your newly purchased safe or a safe deposit box. There should be no reason for you to ever carry your SSN card in your wallet or purse.

Out and about

Tear apart your wallet or purse and reduce the identification information and the number of credit cards you carry. Despite some of the high-tech means we discussed in earlier chapters, the primary way identity thieves get personal information is still from lost or stolen wallets and purses. The fewer things you have in your purse or wallet, the easier it is to ascertain if something is missing.

When you purchase items with a check, don't allow clerks to copy your Social Security number or credit card account information onto the back.

Before you approach an ATM or telephone, be aware of your surroundings. If people are nearby, no matter how innocent they look, consciously shield your calling card and PIN numbers from potential "shoulder surfers." The more public the space, the easier it is for an identity thief to steal these important numbers just by watching your fingers.

They can also listen near a public phone while you're giving out a credit card number to reserve a hotel room, rent a car, purchase tickets, or guarantee a restaurant reservation. If you must call someone from a public phone, especially if you need to pass on personal financial information to the person you're calling, use a telephone booth where you can close the door, or find a less public location. The same rules apply to cell phone use. Find a quiet, private place to minimize eavesdropping.

Online

Just as you need to be wary when asked to supply personal information on the phone, you shouldn't do it online unless you've gone to the site and you're familiar with whom you're dealing. Never purchase anything from a merchant without a secure server. These sites begin with "**https**" instead of "http" or "www."

Take the security of your computer seriously. Make sure your virus protection is kept up-to-date. Install a firewall to make it more difficult for hackers to get into your system. This is particularly essential if you use a cable modem, DSL, T-1, or any other connection that is "always on." And use a secure browser.

Don't store sensitive financial data on your computer if you can avoid it, especially on a laptop.

And when you dispose of your computer, make sure you make all data impossible to recover—it may not be enough to just delete it.

At work

Find out who has access to your personal information at work and verify that the records are kept in a secure location.

Ask your employer, school, and others *not* to use your Social Security number as a personal identifier.

If you keep important records at work—accounting, medical, taxes, etc.—make sure they are secure.

Your mail

According to the FTC, stealing mail is the second most successful means for getting identity information (after wallets and purses). Guard your mail from theft. Deposit outgoing mail in post office collection boxes or at your local post office. Promptly remove mail from your mailbox after it has been delivered.

If you live in the U.S. and are planning to be away from home and can't pick up your mail, call the U.S. Postal Service at 1-800-275-8777 to request a vacation hold. The Postal Service will hold your mail at your local post office until you can pick it up. Consider using a P.O. box or mail receiving service (for example, Mailboxes Etc.) for receiving mail. Alternatively, have a close friend or relative pick up and hold your mail while you're on a vacation or business trip.

C **Check your credit card, bank, brokerage, and other financial accounts regularly. Look for what should be there and what shouldn't.**

Cancel the credit cards you rarely use. Why have more numbers—and more unused credit—out there for someone to access?

CardCops, an anti-fraud education group, has identified nearly 100,000 credit card numbers that may already have been stolen. Go to *www.Cardcops.com* and type in your credit card number to see if it has already been fraudulently used.[2]

Pay particular attention to your billing cycles. Follow up with creditors if your bills don't arrive on time. A missing credit card bill could mean an identity thief has taken over your credit card account and changed your billing address to cover his tracks.

Checking your monthly statements carefully may be the quickest way for you to uncover the theft. If you're *not* receiving monthly statements for one or more accounts, call the financial institution or credit card company immediately. If you're told that your statements are being mailed to another address, make it clear that you did *not* authorize the change of address and that someone may be improperly using your accounts. Then ask for copies of all statements and debit or charge transactions that have occurred since the last statement you received.

Ask for a copy of your credit report, from each of the three major credit reporting agencies, at least once a year.

Order a copy of your credit report from each of the three major credit reporting agencies at least once a year. Make sure they are accurate and include only those activities you've authorized. If you are a fraud victim, have been denied credit within the past 60 days, or are a resident of Colorado, Georgia, Massachusetts, Maryland, New Jersey, or Vermont, the bureau will provide you with a free copy of your report. Otherwise, the law allows credit bureaus to charge you up to $9 for a copy of your credit report (more if you order online):

Equifax	Experian	TransUnion
800-685-1111	888-397-3742	800-888-4213
www.equifax.com	*www.experian.com*	*www.transunion.com*

Your credit report contains information on where you work and live, the credit accounts that have been opened in your name, how you pay your bills, and whether you've been sued, arrested, or filed for bankruptcy. Checking these reports on a regular basis can help you catch mistakes and fraud before they wreak havoc on your personal finances.

Maintain careful records of your banking and financial accounts.

Even though financial institutions are required to maintain copies of your checks, debit transactions, and similar transactions for five years, you should retain your own copies of monthly statements and checks. If you need to dispute a particular check or transaction—especially one a financial institution claims bears *your* signature—your original records may prove invaluable.

Other important steps to take

Treat prescreened credit card offers and convenience checks like blank checks—as we've seen in previous chapters, identity thieves certainly appreciate their value. Tear them up or shred them if you don't plan to accept them or use them, or they may well be used—by someone else—without your knowledge.

The three major credit bureaus use the same toll-free number to let consumers choose not to receive prescreened credit offers. Call 888-5-OPTOUT (888-567-8688).

Of the three major credit bureaus, only Experian offers consumers the ability to remove their names from lists used for marketing and promotional purposes. Call 800-407-1088.

The Direct Marketing Association's (DMA) Mail, E-mail and Telephone Preference Services allow consumers to opt out of direct mail marketing, e-mail marketing, and/or telemarketing solicitations from many national companies. Because your name will not be on their lists, it also means that these companies can't rent or sell your name to still more companies.

To remove your name from many national direct mail lists, write to:

> Direct Marketing Association
> P.O. Box 643
> Carmel, NY 10512
> Or go online ($5 charge):
> *www.the-dma.org/consumers/offmailinglist.html*

To remove your e-mail address from many national direct e-mail lists, go to *www.dmaconsumers.org/offemaillist.html*.

To avoid unwanted phone calls from many national marketers, send your name, address, and telephone number to:

> Direct Marketing Association
> Telephone Preference Service
> PO Box 1559
> Carmel, NY 10512
> Or go online ($5 charge):
> *www.the-dma.org/consumers/offtelephonelist.html*

As an earlier true-life example pointed out, there *is* no Federal "do not call" registry, but you may be able to register with your state. Information on each state's policies and procedures is available at *www.ftc.gov/donotcall*. Whether you may (or if you do) register with your state, you should tell any telemarketer that calls you wish to be placed on *their* "do not call" list. Federal law requires them to honor your request.

Just remember, when all is said and done, following these steps will significantly reduce the chance that an identity thief will target you...or be successful if he does. There is simply no way to completely *eliminate* that risk. A case in point:

North Little Rock, Arkansas, police are still looking for a man who managed to obtain three state identification cards with the same picture but under different names. "To obtain them," according to police, "[he] used no more information than he could have found in a phone book."

"The advice usually [offered by Joyce Lanoue, a spokesperson for the Social Security Administration], such as not carrying around a Social Security card or putting the number on a driver's license and shredding personal papers, would not have helped."[3]

Are You at Risk for Identity Theft?
The Identity Theft IQ Test

Test your "Identity Quotient."

❑ I receive several offers of pre-approved credit every week. (5 points)

❑ Add 5 more points if you do not shred them before putting them in the trash.

❑ I carry my Social Security card in my wallet. (10 points)

❑ My state driver's license has my SSN printed on it, and I have not contacted the Department of Motor Vehicles to request a different number. (10 points)

❑ I do not have a PO Box or a locked, secured mailbox. (5 points)

❑ I use an unlocked, open box at work or at my home to drop off my outgoing mail. (10 points)

❑ I carry my military ID in my wallet at all times. (10 points)

❑ I do not shred or tear banking and credit information when I throw it in the trash. (10 points)

❑ I provide my Social Security number (SSN) whenever asked, without asking questions as to how that information will be safeguarded. (10 points)

❑ Add 5 points if you provide it orally without checking to see who might be listening.

❑ I am required to use my SSN at work as an employee ID or at college as a student ID number. (5 points)

❑ My SSN is printed on my employee badge that I wear at work or in public. Or it is posted on my time card in full view of others, or is on other documents frequently seen by many others in my workplace. (10 points)

❏ I have my SSN and/or driver's license number printed on my personal checks. (10 points)

❏ I am listed in a "Who's Who" guide. (5 points)

❏ I carry my insurance card in my wallet and either my SSN or that of my spouse is the ID number. (10 points)

❏ I have not ordered a copy of my credit reports for at least 2 years. (20 points)

❏ I do not believe that people would root around in my trash looking for credit or financial information. (10 points)

Each one of these questions represents a possible avenue for an identity thief.

100 + points:	You are at high risk. We recommend you purchase a paper shredder, become more security-aware in document handling and start to question why people need your personal data.
50-100 points:	Your odds of being victimized are about average, higher if you have good credit.
0-50 points:	Congratulations. You have a high "IQ." Keep up the good work, and don't let your guard down now.

The Identity Theft IQ Test was developed by the Privacy Rights Clearinghouse, *www.privacyrights.org*, and the Utility Consumers' Action Network, *www.ucan.org*. Used with permission of the Privacy Rights Clearinghouse.

Chapter

The Law Is (Finally) on Your Side

"This [is] a crime that has not been taken terribly seriously until recently."

—Senator Diane Feinstein[1]

The Federal government finally started taking identity theft seriously in October 1998, when The Identity Theft and Assumption Deterrence Act was enacted.

Why was it needed? Because the statute it amended (18 U.S.C. § 1028) only dealt with "the fraudulent creation, use, or transfer of identification *documents," not* the theft of the underlying personal information. So, the effect of the Identity Theft Act was to criminalize the theft or misuse of personal identifying information, *regardless of whether it appears or is used in documents*.

Specifically, the Act made it unlawful for anyone who "knowingly transfers or uses, without lawful authority, a means of identification of another person with the intent to commit, or to aid or abet, any unlawful activity that constitutes a violation of Federal law, or that constitutes a felony under any applicable

State or local law." Note that a name or Social Security number is considered a means of identification, as is a credit card number, cellular telephone electronic serial number, or any other piece of information that may be used to identify a specific individual.

Penalties were also increased. The Identity Theft Act provides for a term of imprisonment of not more than 15 years "when an individual commits an offense that involves the transfer or use of one or more means of identification if, as a result of the offense, anything of value aggregating $1,000 or more during any one year period is obtained."

And *attempted* identity theft is subject to the same penalties as the offense itself.

Penalties are even more stringent under certain circumstances: "If the offense is committed to facilitate a drug trafficking crime, or in connection with a crime of violence, or is committed by a person previously convicted of identity theft, the individual is subject to a term of imprisonment of not more than 20 years." And a section was added that provides for the forfeiture of any personal property used (or intended to be used) to commit the offense.

In addition, to ensure that identity thieves receive appropriately severe sentences, the United States Sentencing Commission issued specific Sentencing Guidelines for identity theft, which, among other enhancements, set a "floor"—that is, a minimum offense level—which ensures that even a person with no prior criminal convictions could get a prison sentence of at least 10-16 months. The Guidelines also invite upward "departures" for more severe sentences where egregious conduct seriously affects individuals (for example, where the criminal takes over an innocent victim's identity).[2]

Violations of the Identity Theft Act are investigated by the Federal Bureau of Investigation; the Secret Service, for bank and credit card fraud; the U.S. Postal Inspection Service, for mail fraud; the Social Security Administration's Office of Inspector

General, for fraud relating to Social Security benefits; and the Internal Revenue Service, for tax fraud. The Justice Department handles the prosecution of cases under the Identity Theft Act.[3]

To help coordinate identity theft investigation and prosecution, the Justice Department created a working group that includes representatives from its own Criminal Division, the U.S. Trustees, the FBI, the FTC, the Secret Service, U.S. Postal Inspection Service, IRS, Social Security Administration; and state and local governments.[4]

The Act also required the Federal Trade Commission to "log and acknowledge the receipt of complaints by individuals who certify that they have a reasonable belief that one or more of their means of identification have been assumed, stolen, or otherwise unlawfully acquired."

In November 1999, the FTC established the Identity Theft Data Clearinghouse for consumer complaints and questions. Law enforcement organizations that were members of the Consumer Sentinel Network (the FTC's universal fraud complaint database) gained access to the Clearinghouse in July of 2000.[5]

In its first month of operation, the Clearinghouse answered an average of 445 calls per week. By March 2001, the average had increased to over 2,000 calls per week. In December 2001, the weekly average was 3,000.[6] The database now contains more than 170,000 consumer complaints. What is truly frightening is that the FTC estimates that this *represents less than 10 percent of the actual number of identity theft victims.*

In 2001, the FTC revealed that identity theft accounted for 42 percent of *all* complaints it received, far more than any other category of consumer fraud.

Law enforcement agencies now utilize the Clearinghouse in two ways: to initiate new investigations, and even more often, to identify additional victims, suspects, addresses, phone numbers, and criminal activities related to an ongoing investigation.

Since the inception of the Clearinghouse, 46 separate federal agencies and 306 different state and local agencies have signed up for access, including more than half the state Attorneys General and law enforcement from Baltimore, Dallas, Los Angeles, Miami, San Francisco, and Philadelphia.

While this important legislation has been a large factor in law enforcement's ability to prosecute identity thieves and mete out far more severe sentences than previously, it has little to do with the practical problems consumers face when their identity is stolen or compromised. Three other longstanding laws are more pertinent:

The Fair Credit Reporting Act[7]

The federal Fair Credit Reporting Act (FCRA) was designed to promote accuracy, fairness, and privacy of information in the files of consumer reporting agencies (CRAs) such as Experian, Equifax, and Transunion (the big three), and their ilk. It gives you very specific rights:

You must be told if information in your file has been used against you. Anyone who uses information from a CRA to take action against you—such as denying an application for credit, insurance, or employment—must tell you, and give you the name, address, and phone number of the CRA that gave them the information.

You can find out what is in your file. At your request, a CRA *must* give you the information in your file and a list of everyone who has requested it recently. They may charge up to $9 for each report (unless you live in Colorado, Georgia, Massachusetts, Maryland, New Jersey, or Vermont, in which case you get one free report per year).

You can dispute inaccurate information with the CRA. The CRA *must* investigate the items you question (usually within 30 days) by presenting your evidence to whomever supplied the information. The source must review your evidence and report its findings to the CRA. The CRA must give you a written report of the investigation and a copy of your report if the investigation results in any change.

If the CRA's investigation does not resolve the dispute, you may add a brief statement to your file. The CRA must normally include a summary of your statement in future reports. If an item is deleted or a dispute statement is filed, you may ask that anyone who has recently received your report be notified of the change.

Inaccurate information must be corrected or deleted... usually within 30 days after you dispute it. If your dispute results in any change to your report, the CRA cannot reinsert a disputed item into your file unless the information source verifies its accuracy and completeness. In addition, the CRA must give you a written notice telling you it has reinserted the item and with whom it verified the information.

You can dispute inaccurate items with the source of the information. If you tell anyone—such as a creditor who reports to a CRA—that you dispute an item, they may not report the information to a CRA without including a notice that you dispute the information.

Outdated information may not be reported. In most cases, a CRA may not report negative information that is more than seven years old; 10 years old for bankruptcies.

Access to your file is limited. A CRA may provide information about you only to people with a need recognized by the FCRA, usually to consider an application with a creditor, insurer, employer, landlord, or other business.

Your consent is required for reports that are provided to employers and for reports that contain medical information. A CRA may not give out information about you to an employer or *prospective* employer without your written consent. And it may not report medical information to creditors, insurers, or employers without your permission.

You may choose to exclude your name from CRA lists for unsolicited credit and insurance offers. If you call the toll-free number that must appear on any such mailing and ask to be excluded in the future, you must be kept off the lists for two years. If you request, complete, and return the appropriate CRA form, you can remove yourself from the lists *forever*.

You may seek damages from violators. If a CRA, a user, or (in some cases) a provider of CRA data violates the FCRA, you may sue them in state or federal court.

Fair Credit Billing Act[8]

The Fair Credit Billing Act (FCBA) applies to "open end" credit accounts, such as credit cards, and revolving charge accounts, such as department store accounts. It does not cover installment contracts—loans or extensions of credit you repay on a fixed schedule. Nevertheless, if a thief has appropriated your credit cards or opened new accounts in your name, the FCBA's provisions give you some important rights.

The FCBA settlement procedures apply only to disputes about billing errors: Unauthorized charges (Federal law limits your liability to $50); charges that list the wrong date or amount; charges for goods and services you didn't accept or weren't delivered as agreed; math errors; failure to post payments and other credits, such as returns; failure to send bills to your current address; and charges for which you ask for an explanation or written proof of purchase along with a claimed error or request for clarification.

You may withhold payment on any disputed amount (and related charges), during its investigation. You must pay any part of the bill not in question, including finance charges on the undisputed amount.

The creditor may not take any legal or other action to collect the disputed amount and related charges (including finance charges) during the investigation. While your account cannot be closed or restricted, the disputed amount may be applied against your credit limit.

The creditor may not threaten your credit rating or report you as delinquent while your bill is in dispute. However, the creditor may report that you are challenging your bill. In addition, the Equal Credit Opportunity Act prohibits creditors from discriminating against credit applicants who exercise their rights, in good faith, under the FCBA. In other words, you cannot be denied credit simply because you've disputed a bill.

FCBA violations should be reported to the Federal Trade Commission (877-FTC-HELP).

Electronic Fund Transfer Act[9]

The Federal Electronic Fund Transfer Act covers ATMs (Automated Teller Machines), Direct Deposit, Pay-by-Phone systems, and electronic systems that let you pay with a debit card.

Before you contract for EFT services or make your first electronic transfer, the institution must give you the following information:

▶ A summary of your liability for unauthorized transfers.

▶ The telephone number and address of the person to be notified if you think an unauthorized transfer has been or may be made; a statement of the institution's "business days" (when they're open for business); and the number of days you have to report suspected unauthorized transfers.

▶ The type of transfers you can make, fees for transfers, and any limits on the frequency and dollar amount of transfers.

▶ A summary of your right to receive documentation of transfers, to stop payment on a pre-authorized transfer, and the procedures to follow to stop payment.

▶ A notice describing the procedures you must follow to report an error on a receipt for an EFT or your periodic statement, to request more information about a transfer listed on your statement, and how long you have to make your report.

▶ A summary of the institution's liability to you if it fails to make or stop certain transactions.

▶ Circumstances under which the institution will disclose information to third parties concerning your account.

▶ A notice that you may be charged a fee by ATMs where you don't have an account.

Yes, you got all this the first time you opened your bank account or got a debit card, but it was all in small print and you threw it out, didn't you? You may want to request it again, just so you know what to do in the case of fraudulent use of your debit card or shenanigans with your bank account, either through checks or an ATM.

You have 60 days from the date a problem or error appears on your statement or terminal receipt to notify your financial institution. If you fail to do so, you may have little recourse. Under federal law, the institution has no obligation to conduct an investigation if you've missed the 60-day deadline.

An error also may occur in connection with a point-of-sale purchase with a debit card. Once you've notified the company about the error, it has 10 business days to investigate and tell you the results.

If your credit card is lost or stolen, you can't lose more than $50. If someone uses your ATM or debit card without your permission, you can lose much more, depending on how quickly you report its loss.

If you report an ATM or debit card missing to the card issuer before it's used without your permission, you can't be held responsible for any unauthorized withdrawals.

If you report the loss within two business days, you won't be responsible for more than $50. If you report it after two business days but no later than 60 days after your statement is mailed to you, you could lose as much as $500.

If you fail to report an unauthorized transfer within 60 days after your statement is mailed to you, you risk unlimited loss— all the money in your account *and* the unused portion of your maximum line of credit established for overdrafts. (However, VISA and MasterCard have voluntarily agreed to limit consumers' liability for unauthorized use of *their* debit cards to $50 per card, no matter how much time has elapsed since the discovery of the loss or theft.)

Once you report the loss or theft of your ATM or debit card, you're no longer responsible for unauthorized transfers that occur after that time. Because these unauthorized transfers may appear on your statements, however, you should carefully review each statement you receive after you've reported the loss or theft.

Other Federal legislation

After lolling behind the eight ball for so long, law enforcement has clearly gotten the message: Identity theft is costing hundreds of millions of dollars and affecting hundreds of thousands of people a year. Although the Identity Theft and Deterrence Act is a good general piece of legislation, there is still a need for legislation that helps close some of the doors through which identity thieves can so easily walk.

There are concerned legislators who are trying. For example, in May 2002, Congressmen Jim Moran and Tom Davis proposed The Driver's License Modernization Act, which would establish standardized security features for all state-issued drivers' licenses.[10] Among other things, it would:

♦ Require a biometric feature, such as a retinal scan or fingerprint, on an encrypted smart chip embedded in new drivers' licenses.

- ◆ Require all DMV databases to be linked, allowing one state to verify the identity of an applicant from another state.

- ◆ Require states to set tougher standards for the "breeder documents" (birth certificate or other identification) it requires people to submit to apply for drivers' licenses.

- ◆ Make it a federal crime to alter or create a fake driver's license.

In November 2001, the Restore Your Identity Act of 2001 (S 1742) was introduced, though it has not yet been passed. The two most important provisions:

▸ It makes it far easier for victims to get the supporting documents they often need to prove that identity theft has actually occurred.

▸ It amends the Fair Credit Reporting Act to give consumers the power to "permanently block the reporting of any information...resulting from identity theft..." and force the credit bureaus to "notify the furnisher of information identified by the consumer that the information may be a result of identity theft, that a police report has been filed, that a block has been requested...and the effective date of the block."

Despite these efforts, we are not ready (nor may we ever be) to pass the kind of legislation that could strike a death blow against identity theft. Canada, on the other hand, recently passed the Personal Information Protection and Electronic Documents Act, which prohibits any entity from collecting *any* personal information on someone without his or her consent and putting it to commercial use. If enacted in the U.S., this legislation would effectively kill all data warehouses, Internet information brokers and the credit reporting agencies.

Don't hold your breath.

Your state is probably trying to protect you, too

The following are some of the state laws dealing with identity theft. Check with your own state attorney general's office for more information on the protections offered in your state. A summary of all state laws is available at *www.consumer.gov/ idtheft/statelaw.html*, from which this most current information was extracted:

Alabama	2001 Al. Pub. Act 312; 2001 Al. SB 144
Alaska	Stat § 11.46.180
Arizona	Ariz. Rev. Stat. § 13-2008
Arkansas	Ark. Code Ann. § 5-37-227
California	Cal. Penal Code § 530.5-530.7
Colorado	Colo. Rev. Stat. § 18-5-102 & 113
Connecticut	1999 Gen. Stat. § 53(a)-129(a)
Delaware	Del. Code Ann. tit. II, § 854
Florida	Fla. Stat. Ann. § 817.568
Georgia	Ga. Code Ann. §§ 16-9-121, 16-9-127
Hawaii	Haw. Rev. Stat. § 708-810z
Idaho	Rev. Stat. § 708-8102 Idaho Code § 18-3126
Illinois	720 Ill. Comp. Stat. 5/16 G
Indiana	Ind. Code Ann. § 35-43-5-4 (2000)
Iowa	Iowa Code § 715A.8
Kansas	Kan. Stat. Ann. § 21-4018
Kentucky	Ky. Rev. Stat. Ann. § 514.160
Louisiana	La. Rev. Stat. Ann. § 14:67.16
Maine	Me. Rev. Stat. Ann. § tit. 17-A, § 354-2A
Maryland	Md. Ann. Code art. 27, § 231
Massachusetts	Mass. Gen. Laws ch. 266, § 37E

Michigan	Mich. Comp. Laws § 750.285
Minnesota	Minn. Stat. Ann. § 609.527
Mississippi	Miss. Code Ann. § 97-19-85
Missouri	Mo. Rev. Stat. § 570.223
Montana	H.B. 331, 2001 Leg. (not yet codified)
Nevada	Nev. Rev. Stat. § 205.463-465
New Hampshire	N.H. Rev. Stat. Ann. § 638:26
New Jersey	N.J. Stat. Ann. § 2C:21-17
New Mexico	HB317, 2001 Leg. 45th Sess.
North Carolina	N.C. Gen. Stat. § 14-113.20
North Dakota	N.D.C.C. § 12.1-23
Ohio	Ohio Rev. Code Ann. 2913.49
Oklahoma	Okla. Stat. tit. 21, § 1533.1
Oregon	Or. Rev. Stat. § 165.800
Pennsylvania	18 Pa. Cons. State § 4120
Rhode Island	R.I. Gen. Laws § 11-49.1-1
South Carolina	S.C. Code Ann. § 16-13-500, 501
South Dakota	S.D. Codified Laws § 22-30A-3.1.
Tennessee	Tenn. Code Ann. § 39-14-150
Texas	Tex. Penal Code § 32.51
Utah	Utah Code Ann. § 76-6-1101-1104
Virginia	VA. Code Ann. § 18.2-186.3
Washington	Wash. Rev. Code § 9.35.020
West Virginia	W. Va. Code § 61-3-54
Wisconsin	Wis. Stat. § 943.201
Wyoming	Wyo. Stat. Ann. § 6-3-901
Guam	9 Guam Code Ann. § 46.80
U.S. Virgin Islands	14 VI Code Ann. §§ 3003

Chapter

8

What to Do If You're a Victim

No matter how careful you've been, there is simply no way to eliminate the risk of identity theft. If you think *your* name or important personal information has been hijacked, go on the offensive—take immediate action, and keep a detailed record of your conversations and correspondence.

Your step-by-step action guide

▶ **Contact the fraud departments of each of the three major credit bureaus.**

Tell them you're an identity-theft victim and request that a "fraud alert" be placed in your file, as well as a victim's statement asking creditors to call you before opening any new accounts or changing anything involving your existing accounts. While the bureaus may only include a fraud alert for 60 to 90 days, you may request that it be included for up to seven years.[1]

As anyone who has ever tried to correct erroneous information on a credit report knows, the bureaus are much better at collecting the information than they are at ensuring its accuracy. So don't assume that notifying them will automatically stop someone from opening new accounts.

▶ **Order copies of your credit reports from all three major bureaus**

If you claim your credit report is inaccurate because of fraud, the credit bureaus must give you a free report when you request it in writing. Review your reports carefully to make sure no additional fraudulent accounts have been opened in your name and no unauthorized changes made to your existing accounts. Also, check the section of your report that lists "inquiries." Request that any such listings from companies that opened fraudulent accounts be removed.

In a few months—and every six months thereafter—order new copies of your reports to verify that the corrections and changes have actually been made, and to make sure no new fraudulent activity has occurred.

▶ **Close any credit or financial accounts that have been tampered with...**

...and open new ones with different Personal Identification Numbers (PINs) and passwords.

▶ **File a report with your local police...**

...or the police in the community where the identity theft took place.

Get a copy of the police report in case a bank, credit card company or other creditor needs proof of the crime. Even if the police can't catch the identity thief who victimized you, having a copy of the police report may be necessary when dealing with creditors, some of whom may still assume you're just trying to get out of paying a legitimate debt.

▶ Fill out and file an ID Theft Affidavit

The complete form and instructions for completing the affidavit are included in Appendix E. All three credit bureaus accept this form, as do numerous other companies, including AT&T, Bank of America, Bankers Trust, Capital One, Chase Manhattan Bank, FleetBoston, Merrill Lynch, Providian, and Sears. Make sure you also call the FTC's ID Theft Hotline: 877-IDTHEFT. While the FTC has no specific enforcement duties, Federal and state agencies can utilize the information collected in the FTC Clearinghouse.

▶ After calling the credit bureaus, follow up in writing

Tell them what information you believe is inaccurate. Include copies (*not* originals) of documents that support your position. In addition to providing your complete name and address, your letter should clearly identify each disputed item, explain why you dispute it, and request its deletion or correction. You may want to enclose a copy of your credit report with the disputed items *circled*. Send your letter by certified mail. Request a return receipt so you can document what the credit bureau received and when. Keep copies of all correspondence.

Credit bureaus must investigate the items you question, usually within 30 days. They also must forward all relevant data you provide about the dispute to whomever gave them the information in the first place—credit card companies, phone companies and other utilities, or banks and other lenders. After the creditor receives notice of a dispute from the credit bureau, it must investigate, review all relevant information provided by the credit bureau, report back the results of its investigation and identify information it has learned is inaccurate. You have some very important rights in this area:

- ◆ Disputed information that cannot be verified must be deleted from your file.

◆ If your report contains erroneous information, the credit bureau must correct it.

◆ If an item is incomplete, the credit bureau must complete it. For example, if your file shows that you have been late making payments, but fails to show that you are no longer delinquent, the credit bureau must show that you're current.

◆ If your file shows an account belongs to someone else, the credit bureau must delete it.

When the investigation is complete, the credit bureau must give you the written results and a free copy of your report if the dispute results in a change. If an item is changed or removed, the credit bureau cannot put the disputed information back in your file unless a creditor verifies its accuracy and completeness, and the credit bureau gives you a written notice that includes the name, address and phone number of the company providing the information.

If you request, the credit bureau must send notices of corrections to anyone who received your report in the past six months. Job applicants can have a corrected copy of their report sent to anyone who received it for employment purposes during the past two years. If an investigation does not resolve your dispute, ask the credit bureau to include your statement of the dispute in your file and in future reports.

▶ **Notify creditors of disputed items**

Ask to speak with someone in the security or fraud department of each creditor, and follow up with a letter. It's particularly important to notify credit card companies in writing because that's the consumer protection procedure the law spells out for resolving errors on credit card billing statements.

Again, include copies (*not* originals) of documents that support your position. Many creditors have a specific address for disputes. Once you have contacted the creditor at the correct address, they must include a notice of your dispute when reporting any item to the credit bureaus. In addition, if the disputed information is *not* accurate, a creditor may not use it again.

▶ Don't pay any disputed bills

Paying bills or replacing checks that are not yours, even if that would solve some of the problems caused by the identity thief, may be considered a legal admission that those debts belong to you.[2]

What to do IF...

a thief used one or more of your credit cards:

In most cases, the Truth in Lending Act limits your liability for unauthorized credit card charges to $50 per card. The Fair Credit Billing Act establishes procedures for resolving billing errors on your credit card accounts. To take advantage of the law's consumer protections, you **must**:

◆ Write to the creditor at the address given for "billing inquiries," not the address for sending your payments. Include your name, address, account number, and a description of the billing error, including the amount and date it occurred.

◆ Send your letter so that it reaches the creditor no later than 60 days after the first bill containing the error was mailed to you. If the address on your account was changed by an identity thief and you never received the bill, your dispute letter still must reach the creditor within 60 days of when the creditor *would have* mailed the bill. This is why it's so important to keep track of your billing statements and immediately follow up when any bills don't arrive on time.

♦ Send your letter by certified mail, and request a return receipt. This will be your proof of the date the creditor received the letter. Include copies (*not* originals) of sales slips or other documents that support your position. The creditor must acknowledge your complaint in writing within 30 days after receiving it and resolve the dispute within two billing cycles (but not more than 90 days) after receiving your letter.

your checks were stolen or money was stolen from a bank account:

Close the account and open a new one. Establish a completely new PIN and password. Put stop payments on any checks you are afraid may be fraudulently used. Contact the check verification companies listed below to report stolen checks. SCAN will tell you if an identity thief has been fraudulently using your checks; the latter three accept reports of check fraud directly from consumers:

SCAN: 800-262-7771
TeleCheck: 1-800-710-9898
Certigy: 1-800-437-5120
International Check Services: 800-631-9656

your ATM card was stolen:

It's important to report lost or stolen ATM and debit cards immediately because, as we stressed in the last chapter, the amount you can be held responsible for depends on *how quickly* you report the loss. So call your bank as soon as you notice the theft, and follow up in writing—certified letter, return receipt requested. Keep copies of all correspondence.

Once they've been notified of an error, your bank generally has 10 business days to investigate, three business days to inform you of the results, and one business day to correct an error after determining that one did occur. The bank *may* take up to 45 days to complete its investigation, but *only if* the money in dispute is returned to your account and you are notified promptly of the credit. At the end of the investigation, if no error has been found, the institution may take the money back after sending you a written explanation.

your mail was stolen or a change of address fraudulently filed:

If an identity thief has stolen your mail to get new credit cards, bank and credit card statements, prescreened credit offers, or tax information or filed a change-of-address form, report it to your local postal inspector.

you're afraid someone has stolen your passport...

...or may attempt to obtain one using your personal information: Contact the U.S. Passport Office at *www.travel.state.gov/passport_services.html* or write US Department of State, Passport Services, Consular Lost/Stolen Passport Section, 1111 19th Street, NW, Suite 500, Washington, DC 20036 or call (24 hours/day) 202-955-0292.

a brokerage account has been compromised:

If you believe that an identity thief has tampered with your securities investments or brokerage account(s), immediately report it to your broker or account manager.

You should also file a complaint with the SEC (Securities and Exchange Commission) Complaint Center at *www.sec.gov/complaints.html*. Be sure to include as much detail as possible. Write to them at: SEC Office of Investor Education and Assistance, 450 Fifth Street, NW, Washington, DC 20549-0213, or call 202-942-7040.

an identity thief has established new phone service in your name,...

...and is making unauthorized calls that seem to come from (and are being billed to) your cellular phone, or is using your calling card and PIN: Contact your service provider immediately to cancel the account and/or calling card. Open new accounts and choose new PINs.

If you are having trouble getting fraudulent phone charges removed from your account, contact your state Public Utility Commission for local service providers or the Federal Communications Commission for long distance and cellular providers at *www.fcc.gov/ccb/enforce/complaints.html* or call 888-CALL-FCC.

you believe someone is using your Social Security number:

Report it to the Social Security Administration's Fraud Hotline: 800-269-0271.

Call 800-772-1213 to verify the accuracy of the earnings reported under your Social Security number and to request a copy of your *Social Security Statement*. The Statement lists earnings posted to your Social Security record and provides an estimate of benefits you and your family may be eligible to receive now and in the future. If someone has fraudulently used your Social Security number to get a job, your Statement should alert you.

If you can prove that you're being disadvantaged because someone used your Social Security number, you may request a new one. If you've done all you can to fix the problem and someone is still using your number, under certain circumstances, the Social Security Administration may assign you a new one.

Consider this option carefully. A new SSN may not resolve your identity theft problems; it may actually create new problems. For example, a new SSN does not necessarily ensure a new credit record because credit bureaus may combine the credit records from your old SSN with those from your new one. Even when the old credit information is not associated with your new SSN, the *absence* of any credit history under your new SSN may make it more difficult for you to get credit. And finally, there's no guarantee that your new SSN won't be stolen by an identity thief.

you believe your driver's license was stolen:

Contact your state Department of Motor Vehicles. If your state uses your Social Security number as your driver's license number, ask to substitute another number.

you believe someone has filed for bankruptcy using your name:

Write to the U.S. Trustee in the region where the bankruptcy was filed. A listing of the U.S. Trustee Program's Regions can be found at *www.usdoj.gov/ust*, or in the Blue Pages of your phone book under U.S. Government, Bankruptcy Administration.

Your letter should describe the situation and provide proof of your identity. The U.S. Trustee, if appropriate, will make a referral to criminal law enforcement authorities if you provide appropriate documentation to substantiate your claim. You also may want to file a complaint with the U.S. Attorney and/or the FBI in the city where the bankruptcy was filed.

you believe the identity thief has committed a crime using your name:

In rare instances, an identity thief may create a criminal record using your name. If this happens to you, you may need to hire an attorney to help resolve the problem.

you're being hounded by debt collectors:

The Fair Debt Collection Practices Act prohibits debt collectors from using unfair or deceptive practices to collect overdue bills. You can stop a debt collector from contacting you by writing a letter to the collection agency telling them to stop. Once the debt collector receives your letter, the company may not bother you anymore.

Along with a letter stating you don't owe the money, include copies of all documents that support your position. If you're a victim of identity theft, including a copy (*not* the original) of the police report you filed may be particularly useful.

Key contacts for reporting identity theft

Equifax
P.O. Box 740241, Atlanta, GA 30374-0241
800-525-6285
www.equifax.com

Experian
P.O. Box 9532, Allen, TX 75013
888-EXPERIAN (397-3742)
www.experian.com

TransUnion—Fraud Victim Assistance Division,
P.O. Box 6790, Fullerton, CA 92634
800-680-7289
www.transunion.com

Privacy Rights Clearinghouse
3100 5th Ave., #8, San Diego, CA 92103
619-298-3396
www.privacyrights.org

Identity Theft Resource Center
P. O. Box 26833, San Diego, CA 92196
858-693-7935
www.idtheftcenter.org

U.S. Public Interest Research Group
218 D. St., SE, Washington, DC 20003
202-546-9707
uspirg@pirf.org

Federal Trade Commission
Identity Theft Data Clearinghouse
600 Pennsylvania Ave. NW, Washington, DC 20580
877-438-4338
www.consumer.gov/idtheft

Department of Justice
www.usdoj.gov/criminal/fraud/idtheft.html

Federal Bureau of Investigation
Contact local field office (consult your local telephone directory)
www.ifccfbi.gov

Internal Revenue Service
Taxpayer Advocates Office
877-777-4778
www.treas.gov/irs/ci

Postal Inspection Service
Call your local post office
www.usps.gov/websites/depart/inspect

U.S. Secret Service
Call your local field office
www.treas.gov/usss/financial_crimes.htm

Office of the Inspector General
Social Security Administration
Fraud Hotline
PO Box 17768, Baltimore, MD 21235
800-269-0271
www.ssa.gov
E-mail: oig.hotline@ssa.gov.

Chapter 9

Overcoming the Emotional Impact of Identity Theft

By Linda Foley
Executive Director, Identity Theft Resource Center

You've been spending hours writing to credit card companies, calling merchants, and waiting on hold with credit bureaus so you can report the crime and request your credit report. Each time you answer the telephone or go to the mailbox, you wonder what new bill will appear. The idea of dealing with yet another collection agency or with a newly discovered credit card leaves you filled with dread, rage, and helplessness.

It is *normal* for this crime to have an emotional impact on you and your family. In fact, it would be *unusual* if it did not.

Identity theft is a complex problem. Therefore, it is not surprising that some victims react as survivors of prolonged, repeated trauma, much like battered women or prisoners of war. In fact, victims may compare the crime to rape or torture. Some feel like they are experiencing a form of post-traumatic stress disorder for a short time.

At one point or another, victims of identity theft may feel overwhelmed by the psychological pain of loss, helplessness, anger, isolation, betrayal, rage, and even embarrassment. This crime triggers deep fears regarding financial security, the safety of family members, and the ability to ever trust again.

It is not uncommon for identity theft victims to shut down emotionally and withdraw from family, friends, and co-workers. You might suspect that someone you know committed this crime or perhaps you might feel that no one seems to care or understand how devastated you are by the crime. Let's face it, many friends and family members get tired of hearing about the crime after the first or second time. The fact is, though, that it may take months for it to be completely cleared and you may want to talk about it for more than a couple of days.

Dealing with the mess left by an imposter is only part of your job. This crime, like other long-term crimes that involve repeated emotional abuse, can affect not only *your* emotional stability but that of your family as well. So, while you take care of the paperwork, don't forget to leave a little time to work on healing your and your family's emotional wounds.

The moment of discovery

Be prepared for a roller coaster ride of emotions. As the implications sink in you may well find yourself cycling between denial (*This is not happening!*), rage (*How dare they!*), endless questioning (*How is this possible? Why me?*), and hopelessness and vulnerability (*Nothing can protect me.*). This is normal and should be expected. Few people are emotionally protected from the impact of identity theft. There is a profound loss of innocence and trust associated with this crime. You may also have to deal with the fact that someone you personally know may be involved in the theft. That's a lot to absorb.

Finally, you may feel stonewalled by the very people you turn to for help: the police and criminal justice system. Identity theft is a difficult crime to solve and the wheels of justice are still very squeaky. Be patient with yourself and with those who want to help.

Starting the healing process

While it might take some time to straighten out the paper trail, it is important for you to regain your emotional balance as quickly as possible. The feelings you have are valid. You have been harmed. Recognizing and accepting your fears, apprehensions, and frustrations are a first step. They might even sneak up on you, unexpected, sometimes long after the original crime, triggered by a situation most people would just shrug off. Don't berate yourself. Such emotional floods are a part of the healing process.

Embarrassment: A waste of time and energy

Some people are embarrassed about becoming an identity theft victim. They feel that they did something wrong or maybe deserved to have this happen to them. No one deserves to be a victim of identity theft. We'll say that again—*No one deserves to be a victim of identity theft*. We all do foolish things. We all have moments we'd give anything to get back and do just the opposite. That's in the past and beating up on yourself will not make this go away. It's wasted energy and you'll need all your strength to clean up your records.

You are not alone

In 2000, there were more than 700,000 new victims of identity theft. Some experts believe that number will exceed one million in 2002. Another expert stated that identity theft happens once every minute. While support and assistance is not as complete as we'd like to see it, there are many resources for victims of identity theft today. You don't need to be alone through this crisis, if you choose not to be.

The value of a support team

The emotional damage and isolation you feel can be compounded if you believe family members or friends don't understand what you are going through. The reality is that people who have not experienced identity theft may not recognize the ongoing nature of this crime. They may feel that after the initial crime, you should just go on with your life, or they may simply tire of hearing about your problem. Many victims find that after they explain how they feel and ask for ongoing support, their support team is more open to being there through the long haul.

Personality changes

It's not surprising that something like identity theft may cause a certain amount of personality change, including the ways you relate to others. Identity theft attacks our innocence and belief in the trustworthiness of others. Some victims go through a period of time when they refuse to give anyone any information. We know of one victim whose employer stole her identity. The victim refused to include her Social Security number and driver's license number on job applications. It took almost six months to find an employer who would interview this "unco-operative" applicant.

Many victims never see the world through the same innocent eyes again. Identity theft is life-altering. However, if you feel the changes have gotten out of hand, or people on your support team raise some concerns, it can be very helpful to seek professional help from someone who understands identity theft response or victimization.

Overcoming feelings of powerlessness

An emotion is your reaction to a situation. While it may not always seem like it, your reaction is under your control. When you say, "He made me angry," you are mentally giving another person your power over your reaction. *He* didn't make you angry. In that split second, without conscious thought, you *chose* to become angry. That awareness is a step in regaining control over the situation.

In terms of paperwork, persistence is the key. Keep track of everyone you talk with and what needs to be done next. Keep a journal with a calendar of "things to do." If you can control the process, you will start to feel more on top of the mess.

Emotionally, at times, it is going to feel like everyone has control of your life but you. You might feel battered and bounced from one person or agency to another in your quest to clear your name. While identity theft seems all-consuming, it is important to acknowledge the other parts of your life that this crime has not touched. Focus on your accomplishments in life, both in the past and in present day.

Finally, some victims find a gift in identity theft. They learn how powerful they truly are. They find an assertiveness they never exercised before. They learn how to talk with high level people and get what they want, sometimes with a boldness they never knew they had. In addition, they discover who their true friends are.

Take time for yourself

Cleaning up the problems left by identity theft can become a full-time job. Take the time to pamper yourself and your support team. Now is the time to take advantage of those two-for-one dinner coupons, offers from others to babysit your kids, help do carpools, or even the housekeeping. This might even be a good time to enjoy a weekend away from town, perhaps with someone you care about. Be kind to yourself. This is not a time to start a new diet. Listen to your body. It will tell you what it needs—rest, a massage, a day at an amusement park, comfort foods (in moderation), a night at a comedy club, or a long bath.

Exercise is a wonderful way to relieve stress and get away from the telephone. Take a long walk in the park, at the beach, or around your favorite lake. Play a round of golf or tennis or even go horseback riding. Swim some laps or go fly a kite. Learn a new sport or hobby.

Finally, don't be afraid to say no to requests for your time. Don't be afraid to speak out when you feel taken advantage of. Identity theft cannot become the only part of your life that you see—do not let it overcome you.

A special note to victims who are financial heads of households

Identity theft plays special havoc on those who are financially responsible for others or who are their own sole source of financial support. This crime threatens your credit rating, may affect your ability to get a loan or purchase a big-ticket item, and even temporarily jeopardizes your existence as you know it. However, please know you have not let your family down. You did not cause this to happen. You are an innocent victim.

We find that being honest with other members of the family takes the unbearable weight from your shoulders. You need to hear them say they don't blame you, and they don't. You have enough to deal with in the paperwork alone. Let your loved ones and friends help with the emotional burden and even some of the paperwork. Few of us can conquer this alone.

Feelings about the imposter(s)

Whether you know the imposter or not, you may give plenty of thought to the person behind the act.

If you know the imposter: You may feel more pronounced feelings of betrayal, especially if the person was a friend or family member. It may be very difficult to turn this person in to the authorities. The decision has many ramifications, for you and for those who know both you and the imposter. You might want to seek counseling, either to help you make your decision or live with its consequences.

If you are a friend/relative of a victim: You need to be supportive. This victim is dealing with much more than a crime. He or she may feel in a no-win situation, especially if the victim is being pulled in two different directions—turn the person in and betray the imposter, or don't act and betray the person insisting on action.

If the imposter is unknown: Victims often report a feeling of insecurity, wondering if the person standing next to them in the market or walking past them on the street may be the imposter. They may distrust everyone, feeling tremendously vulnerable. It's important to put the crime in some sense of proportion in order to function. This may mean focusing on the crime and not the criminal.

To everyone: Making sure the person is arrested may not always bring you peace. Identity theft is epidemic and you are not immune to future crimes by other imposters. An arrest only signifies the imposter's guilt. Peace is yours to create, accept, or deny.

Moving into activism

Some crime victims find that by moving from their personal experience into a broader world, they begin the healing process. Here are some ways that you can help others while helping yourself.

- ◆ Join or begin an identity theft support group.

- ◆ Help other victims.

- ◆ Work to change laws.

- ◆ Increase public awareness.

- ◆ Increase corporate awareness.

- ◆ Help to increase understanding of this crime with law enforcement, district attorneys and victim assistance personnel.

- ◆ Get involved in community volunteer policing programs.

The Identity Theft Resource Center can help you begin a support group, contact one in your area, or become more active in creating public and legislative awareness. You can reach us at voices123@sbcglobal.net or by phone.

Should you consider professional help?

Without intervention, some victims can become so chronically dysfunctional that they are unable to cope any longer. They may be severely depressed. Some symptoms are exhaustion, overeating, anxiousness, drinking, forgetfulness, or an unwillingness to leave home or get out of bed.

Don't wait until you feel lost at the bottom of a pit. Even if you don't feel overwhelmed, talking to a professional can be very beneficial. Going to someone should never be considered a sign of weakness. You are going through a very stressful time and need to talk about your feelings.

Victim assistance professionals have long recognized the value of support groups and counseling for victims of crime— and you are a victim of crime, whether your police department recognizes it as such or not. In some cases, you can seek restitution for the services of a professional therapist should your case go to court.

The following is a partial resource list for those who may not be financially able to afford a private therapist or who may need the name of a good therapy program. We also recommend you look in the front of your local telephone Yellow Pages under Crisis Intervention, Counseling, and Mental Health.

◆ Your religious leader.

◆ Family Service Association.

◆ Your family physician.

◆ YMCA Family Stress Counseling Services.

◆ Your county Mental Health Association.

◆ Senior Citizens: The Agency on Aging and Independence and AARP have referral programs.

◆ Many counties have Victim/Witness Assistance programs affiliated with your local district attorney or police departments. You might also look up a victim assistance unit of your state attorney general's office.

◆ Many professional counseling associations refer clients to free or reduced-cost programs.

◆ Local hospitals often maintain lists of both governmental and nonprofit assistance programs. Some sponsor clinics and support programs. Talk with the mental health department.

◆ Many businesses have an employee assistance program. You may want to talk with your Human Resources representative to find out about availability.

◆ The National Organization of Victim Assistance (NOVA) has a Website (*www.try-nova.org*) and can be contacted for referrals of victim-assistance professionals in your area.

ADDENDUM

Many victims compare identity theft to rape, others to a cancer invading their lives. Many of the symptoms and reactions to identity theft victimization parallel those of violent crime. The following information is for understanding and, perhaps, to reassure victims that what they are experiencing is not abnormal. The reaction to identity theft can run the full spectrum from mild to severe. Clearly, the complexity of the crime itself will also define the severity of the impact, as will any other traumatic events that may occur around that same time frame.

Impact: the moment of discovery

▶ Can last from 2 hours to several days.

▶ Reactions include shock, disbelief, denial, inappropriate laughter, feeling defiled or dirty, shame or embarrassment.

Recoil

▶ Can last for several weeks or months, especially as other instances of theft are uncovered.

▶ Physical and psychological symptoms may include: heart palpitations, chest discomfort, breathing difficulties, shortness of breath, hyperventilation, dizziness, clumsiness, sweating, hot and cold flashes, elevated blood pressure, feeling jumpy or jittery, shaking, diarrhea, easily fatigued, muscle aches, dry mouth, lump in throat, pallor, heightened sensory awareness, headaches, skin rashes, nausea, sexual dysfunction, sleep disturbance.

▶ It is not uncommon for victims to frequently search through events trying to pinpoint what they did to contribute to this crime.

▸ Anger, rage, tearfulness, overwhelming sadness, loss of sense of humor, an inability to concentrate, hyper-protectiveness, and a deep to need withdraw are all part of the psychological reactions to identity theft.

▸ You may misplace anger on others, especially loved ones causing family discord. Those who tend to lean on unhealthy habits such as under- or overeating, smoking, alcohol or drugs may be drawn to those additions for comfort.

▸ During Recoil, victims may experience a sensation of grief. They may grieve the loss of: financial security, sense of fairness, trust in the media, trust in people/humankind and society, trust in law enforcement and criminal justice systems, trust in employer (especially in workplace ID theft), trust in caregivers and loved ones, faith, family equilibrium, sense of invulnerability and sense of safety, hopes/dream and aspirations for the future.

▸ At one point or another, almost all victims will also grieve a loss of innocence, sense of control, sense of empowerment, sense of self and identity, and sense of self worth.

Equilibrium/balance/recovery

▸ In identity theft, this phase may come as early as several weeks after the crime and for others may take months or years. It usually depends on how quickly the actions of the imposter are resolved and cleared up.

▸ For all victims, achieving balance and entering recovery will take awareness and purposeful thought.

Access ITRC at *www.idtheftcenter.org* for current information. A variety of regularly updated fact sheets on identity theft are available.

Chapter

10

When You Know the Identity Thief

By Linda Foley
Executive Director
Identity Theft Resource Center
and
Mari Frank, Esq.
Attorney, Author, and Identity Theft Expert

*The information in this chapter, including the form letters, are **not** to be considered legal advice. This information is a resource for you and has been helpful for other victims in similar situations. However, if you have any legal questions or concerns, you should consult with a consumer law attorney.*

When a Friend, Family Member, Co-Worker, or Ex-Spouse Steals Your Identity: What Are Your Options When You Know the Imposter?

Case 1: *My adult daughter used my information, without my knowledge, to open several credit cards and buy a car. She hasn't paid on any of these accounts and now the bank and credit card companies want me to pay. What do I do? I don't want to see her go to jail.*

Case 2: *My father has a gambling problem. He opened several checking accounts in both my name and my brother's name. Then he wrote bad checks for his debt. He's 68 years old and my family thinks we should just pay off the debt. I know that if we do, he'll just do it again. What do you advise?*

Case 3: *My ex-husband is using my 8-year-old son's SSN to open credit cards. He even got a driver's license using his information. How do I stop him?*

Case 4: *My friend apparently went through my papers one day and found my SSN. She has several credit cards that she applied for in both of our names. I found out when I applied for a card and it was denied. She says she will pay off the cards but can only afford $20 a month. The credit card companies want all of it now. I can't afford to pay these off. It is more than $10,000. What do I do? She won't sign a letter saying these are really her cards because she is afraid they will arrest her.*

Identity theft is a complex crime at best. When the imposter is someone you know, the impact of the crime magnifies dramatically. How do I prosecute my own mother? What kind of father would I be if I allowed the police to arrest my son? Should

I practice "tough love?" What will the other family members think of me? What will my friends say? If the imposter is an ex-spouse, the crime borders on abuse and harassment...

The reality of the situation

Let's look at this situation from various points of view:

The law

If you are the victim of identity theft, you now have the right under federal law and in most states to be considered a victim. If you do not report it, there will be no police report, and no investigation. If you want the protection of the law, you must make a report. You are not an accomplice or co-conspirator unless you knew about the fraud and did nothing to stop it, or if you participated in the fraud yourself. If you refuse to make a report, you may appear suspect when you try to clear the fraud activity (civil or criminal).

Credit card companies and financial institutions

The credit card companies and financial institutions want their money back. That is a reasonable expectation. They know a percentage of people will claim a crime was committed (stolen card or identity theft) in order to get out of paying a bill. One of the standards they have adopted to separate the "deadbeat" from a true case of identity theft is that a person will probably not file a police report if they are making a false claim.

It is your task to convince them that another person has taken over your accounts and/or opened new accounts in your name—all without your permission or knowledge. You will have to prove that you have not benefited financially from these accounts. Unfortunately, without a police report, which some victims do not wish to get, your job will be much tougher. Credit card companies do not take victims as seriously without a police report.

The imposter

There are as many reasons to steal as there are imposters. The imposter may have an emotional problem or addiction that forces them to seek more money than they can afford. Examples are gambling, drugs, shopaholic, or the need for attention. The imposter might be in severe financial straits and decide this is the best way to balance things out.

Some imposters use identity theft to abuse the victim, as in the case of an ex-spouse, former boyfriend/girlfriend or an angry child.

Some imposters do not believe that they have actually harmed the victim. They rationalize that the credit card company will absorb the loss and the victim will be forgiven the debt. The imposter does not realize the emotional and financial impact of this crime or the extensive hours and cost of clearing up compromised financial records. We know of a case of an adult child where the mother has used her identity, and she is now unable to even rent an apartment. She is forced to live at home, with the imposter who created the problem.

The victim

When you personally know the individual who has used your information, the emotional impact of identity theft dramatically increases-the sense of violation and betrayal, embarrassment for yourself and the imposter, the abuse of trust, even your feeling of how you evaluate others. You may feel that this decision is not cut and dry. It has many ramifications, for you and for those who know both you and the imposter. And those who know both of you may put pressure on you to assume the responsibility for the crime to protect the criminal.

One victim put it this way:

"The person who stole my identity was a friend. When I first found out, I was angry at what she did to me, apparently without concern for my feelings or financial security. I reported the situation to the police and then spent the next few weeks worrying about her safety. Would she be arrested? Would she be angry with me? She did get arrested and pled guilty.

The day they took her from the courtroom in shackles was a very difficult day for me. I had a lot of mixed feelings. I knew she would not be able to hurt me for a while, that she would pay for her crime. People told me I should be celebrating. But how do you celebrate when you get to walk in the sunlight and the person you thought was a friend is behind bars, on a cot, alone and unable to feel the breeze on her face?

It took me a while to stop identifying with her. I also had to make peace with myself. I was not the cause of the crime. I was simply a way for her to get money. By going to the police, I had actually given her a gift. A chance to change her ways and get her life together. I finally realized this crime was not about me. It was about her and her problems. I was just an innocent bystander. She was not capable of understanding friendship."

What if you suspect the imposter is someone you know?

What steps can you take to gather the proof you need?

Let's assume you found out by having a credit card refused or having a collection agency call you. The first step is order copies of your credit reports from Experian, TransUnion, and Equifax...We recommend you place a fraud alert at the same time that you order these reports. These reports are free if you believe you might be a victim of financial crime or have been refused credit or a job.

Next, call all the companies or collection agencies that list an account that you have not personally opened or that show a pending application. Let them know this is a case of identity theft and find out what steps you must take to clear their records. Ask these company(ies) for photocopies of the fraudulent applications and credit slips for purchases made. This is very important. With those, you can show that the signature is not yours. You might also recognize the writing, the address used, the purchases made, or the location of purchases. At this time both California and Washington have laws requiring they provide those to you.

Remember, you are not liable for this debt, and the company is taking advantage of the fact that you are a family member if they insist that you pay. We hope you have not paid a penny of the fraudulent credit card accounts. If you have, your case is much harder to fight. Please do not be tempted into paying any of the debt.

Keep trying to get the company to remove the debt. If they won't give you the photocopies of the applications, and if they won't remove the debt from your credit reports, you may have to consider hiring an attorney.

If you live in California, and if you have a police report listing all the fraud accounts, the credit bureaus must block the fraudulent accounts from your credit reports within 30 days. That's the law (California Civil Code 1785.16k). But that means you must file a police report first. If you don't live in California, you should still send a police report to the company(ies) with an attached listing of the fraudulent account(s) demanding that they remove the fraud in 30 days. Once the fraud accounts are removed, they can only be reinserted in your credit profiles if the creditors prove the accounts are not fraudulent. There is a federal law being considered to take this concept nationwide (S1399 Feinstein, March 2002).

Your options

There are many ways in which you can handle this situation:

◆ You can deal with it by deciding not to shield the imposter and report him/her to the credit issuer(s) and to law enforcement.

◆ You can seek mediation, when a third party is hired to help you arrive at a solution that both you and the imposter agree to.

◆ You can also encourage the imposter to seek mental health counseling.

◆ You can deal with the credit issuers yourself.

◆ You can seek legal help.

Or you might choose a combination of all these approaches.

Dealing with the situation

The following are several situations in which you, the victim decide to deal with the matter by not shielding the imposter.

Situation One: Treat this like any other case of ID theft: Go to the authorities. The person who used your information showed a lack of concern for your safety and financial good health. The old saying, "I didn't think it would really hurt you; the credit card companies just write off the loss," cannot be allowed as an excuse. If you have approached that person and told them you have a problem *they* caused and they *don't* respond with an offer to make it completely right immediately, you have been given a loud message. Why would you continue to protect someone who is putting you at risk?

It is difficult, but sometimes the best gift we give someone is to practice "tough love." By contacting the authorities and co-operating fully, you have not caused this person to be arrested. They caused this by their own actions. They have entered a life of crime and by stopping them you may actually prevent them from moving into a more dangerous situation, one that is life threatening. Identity thieves are often repeat offenders. They move from crime to crime, escalating as they continue their behavior.

The imposter will not recognize this gift you have given them now. After therapy and dealing with the court system, they might. They also might never forgive you. In your heart, you must understand you did the right thing, sometimes the most difficult action you will ever take.

Please be careful if you think this person may become violent. Do not confront him [or] her. Speak to law enforcement and make sure you protect yourself.

Situation Two: The imposter admits guilt and will sign a form transferring responsibility from the victim to himself/herself. Contact the credit card company(ies) and let them know about the situation. Send Form Letter 2 [at the end of this chapter], with the affidavit the creditor sends you. We recommend that the imposter provide you with a check in their name for at least 15-25% of the debt to mail with the documents. The check should be made payable to the credit issuer, not you. This shows good intent to the creditors.

Situation Three: The imposter admits theft but will not sign forms. You can try mediation and hope the imposter repays the creditor. To protect yourself, gather documentation about the crime and send Form Letter 1 or use [the ID Theft Affidavit reproduced in Appendix E) along with your police report.

Situation Four: The imposter will not admit guilt and you have conclusive proof of the crime. To protect yourself, gather documentation about the crime and send Form Letter 1 or use [the ID Theft Affidavit reproduced in Appendix E] along with your police report.

Situation Five: The imposter will not admit guilt, you have conclusive proof and the imposter is a repeat offender whom you have confronted prior to this new theft. See Situation One above.

Situation Six: Your whole family tells you to forgive the imposter and they will help you pay off the bills slowly together. Seek mediation and family therapy. Have the family work out an agreement in writing, signed by all parties, to put the debt in the imposter's name to pay it off. See Form Letters 2 and 3.

Situation Seven: The creditor denies that an imposter has stolen your identity despite the proof you have provided or despite admission by the imposter. You believe that the creditor is going to continue to go after you since the imposter does not have any money and you do (the deep pocket theory). In this case we recommend you speak directly with the vice-president of customer service for the company. You might also ask for help from your state attorney general's office or Better Business Bureau claiming unfair business practices.

Situation Eight: The perpetrator is your ex-spouse or soon-to-be ex-spouse. If the person has opened up credit cards in your name, without your authorization, we recommend that you have your divorce attorney address this as part of the divorce proceedings or settlement. If the divorce is final, you may choose to deal with this as in Situation One above or go back to your divorce attorney for additional court assistance—such as a cease and desist order and an order that the perpetrator spouse pay off the debt. Unfortunately, many law enforcement agencies will see this as a continuation of domestic civil action and may not be willing to get involved. Your determination and professionalism in how you deal with the police may sway them to take action. Send a copy of the divorce decree with a cover letter to the creditors and let them go after your ex-spouse.

Mediation

In this situation, you decide to inform your friend or family member that you don't want to be forced to take legal action and therefore are willing to go to a mediator to work out a structured solution and legally binding agreement as to the circumstances. (There are some low-cost community mediation services.) Work out an agreement in writing, signed by all parties, to put the debt in the imposter's name to pay it off. See Form Letters 2 and 3. If the party refuses to cooperate, take whatever action is necessary to protect yourself (for example, a police report).

Therapy

Whatever option you choose, you may want to look into emotional counseling, for yourself, the imposter, and for your family if the imposter is a family member. This is a challenge and all involved must learn "boundaries."

For the victim: It often benefits victims of familial identity theft to talk with a professional, either to help you make your decision or live with its consequences.

For the imposter: This person has issues that need to be identified and dealt with. Possible therapies could include anti-theft counseling, anti-substance abuse counseling (for example, alcohol, drugs, gambling), responsible financial management, developing a conscience, accepting responsibility for one's actions, etc.

For the family or between the victim/friend: The bottom line is that you will eventually all have to live with the consequences of the actions taken by the imposter. You need to talk out your anger (and you will experience anger), open new lines of communication, and see how interactions might have led to this action. You also need to establish boundaries to avoid new cases of abuse/identity theft.

Dealing directly with the credit card companies and/or collection agencies

In this situation, do not lie at any time to any of the companies. If you are not absolutely certain of your imposter's identity, you should *not* make an accusation. It is sufficient to provide all necessary documentation to show that the accounts are not yours.

Situation One: If your imposter admits that he/she obtained the credit in your name, and will take over the account, and if the imposter has no means to pay and has poor credit, the creditor may pressure you, the victim, to keep the account in your name. You must refuse to do this. If the creditor will not transfer the account, it will have to absorb the losses.

Situation Two: If the imposter refuses to accept responsibility, and the creditor knows it is a family member, they cannot force you to make a police report, but they may refuse to accept it as fraud. So you may be forced to file an informational report with the police, or the creditor or company(ies) involved can be the one(s) to file the report. You have the right to ask the creditor to file the report instead of you. However they may refuse to get involved. You must provide evidence of your innocence to law enforcement and the creditors.

Seeking legal assistance

If your impostor has committed crimes in your name, you should definitely contact a criminal defense attorney and have him/her help you to clear your name from the FBI and state criminal records databases. If your family member committed financial fraud, and the creditors will not remove the fraud after you have written letters, you may need to hire a consumer law attorney. For referral, contact the National Association of Consumer Advocates at *www.naca.net* or phone (202) 452-1989. (See The Identity Theft Survival Kit available at *www.identitytheft.org*. It provides additional attorney-written letters on diskette dealing with this situation.)

Form letters

The following are form letters that can be used to attempt to clear your records. These Form Letters are suggestions only and should not take the place of forms or letters provided by your attorney, by law enforcement, or by creditors. All letters should be sent certified, return receipt requested.

▶ Form Letter 1 (see p. 133) letter from victim to credit issuer-may be used when the imposter will not cooperate and will not sign Form Letter Two below. Send a separate form to each creditor. Keep copies copy for yourself.

▶ Form Letter 2 (see p. 137) [should] be written by [an] imposter accepting responsibility for accounts or charges. Use a separate letter for each creditor you are contacting. Keep a copy of each for your records. We recommend that each form (one per fraudulent account) be notarized when the imposter signs it. The imposter should pay for that charge. Make enough copies for each account needed and a few extra for your files. Attach any documentation (e.g. police report) that will help the creditor to deal with this situation.

▶ Form Letter 3: To be used when both parties privately reach an agreement with each other. The [sample included is a suggestion] only. This form will need to be adjusted to reflect your agreements.

Form Letter 1
Affidavit of Fact

Victim Information

My full legal name is

_____

(If different from above) When the events described in this
affidavit took place, I was known as:

_____

My birth date (day/month/year) is _____

My Social Security number is _____

My driver's license or identification card number is:

State _____ # _____

My current address is:

_____

City_____

State_____ Zip Code _____

I have lived at this address since _____
                                              (month/year)

(If different from above) When the events described in this
affidavit took place, my address was:

_____

City_____

State_____ Zip Code _____

I lived at this address from _____

   until _____(month/year)

My daytime telephone number is (____)_____

   Cell (____) _____

My evening telephone number is (____)_____

My e-mail address is _____

How the Fraud Occurred (Check all that apply):

____ I did not authorize anyone to use my name or personal information to seek the money, credit, loans, goods or services described in this report.

____ I did not receive any benefit, money, goods, or services as a result of the events described in this report.

____ My identification documents (i.e., credit cards; birth certificate; driver's license; Social Security card, etc.) _____ were stolen or _____ were lost on or about _____(day/month/year).

____ I have proof that the following person(s) used my information (for example, my name, address, date of birth, existing account numbers, Social Security number, mother's maiden name, etc.) or identification documents to obtain money, credit, loans, goods, or services without my knowledge or authorization: (only fill out if you are certain):

Name(s) (if known)

_____

_____

_____

Address(es) (if known)

_____

_____

_____

Phone number(s) (if known)

_____

_____

_____

Additional information (e.g. relationship), if known

_____

_____

_____

A report has been made with the following police/sheriff's department. If you are unable to obtain a report or report number from the police, please indicate that by checking here _____.

Name of agency:

_____

Name of investigator, if known:

_____

Contact information for law enforcement:

_____

_____

_____

I declare under penalty of perjury that this declaration is true and correct to the best of my knowledge.

Signature of victim

Date

Knowingly submitting false information on this affidavit could subject you to criminal prosecution for perjury.

Have one witness (non-relative) sign below that you completed and signed this declaration.

Witness:

---
signature

---
printed name

---
date, telephone number

Form Letter 2

My name is (full legal name):

_____

This is to notify you that (check all that apply):

____ I opened the following credit account(s) in the victim's name.

____ I added charges onto an existing credit card account owned by the victim.

____ I took over a bank account or checking account owned by the victim.

____ I opened a bank account or checking account in the victim's name.

Account number(s) of fraudulent account(s):

_____

_____

_____

_____

Date each opened:

_____

_____

_____

_____

Approximate amount of charges to date:

_____

Social Security number used to open account:

_____

Legal authorization: (have imposter initial each):

___ The victim did not authorize me to use his/her name or personal information to seek the money, credit, loans, goods or services described in this report.

___ The victim did not have any knowledge of my actions described in this report.

___ The victim did not receive any benefit, money, goods, or services as a result of the events described in this report.

___ A police report has been filed about this situation.
___ Yes (attached) ___ No

___ I wish to assume full financial responsibility for all charges made by me in the name of the victim and contact me exclusively to make arrangements for repayment of these charges. I also request that a written confirmation be sent to the victim showing:

1. That all fraudulent charges have been removed from their records within your company.

2. That the credit bureaus Experian, Equifax and TransUnion have been contacted to remove the fraudulent account/charges from their records.

Imposter Information

My full legal name is:

_____

When the events described in this affidavit took place, my name was: _____

My Social Security number is: _____

My driver's license number is:

State _____ # _____

My current address is:

_____

City_____

State_____ Zip Code_____

I have lived at this address since _____
                                                    (month/year)

(If different from above) When the events described in this affidavit took place, my address was:

_____

City_____

State_____ Zip Code_____

My daytime telephone number is (____)_____

    Cell (____)_____

My evening telephone number is (____)_____

My e-mail address is _____

Victim Information

Victim's full legal name:

_____

Victim's address:

_____

_____

_____

Victim's telephone number:

Home (____)_____ Work (____)_____

Victim's Social Security Number:

_____

I declare under penalty of perjury that this declaration is true and correct to the best of my knowledge.

_____
Signature of victim

_____
Date

I declare under penalty of perjury that this declaration is true and correct to the best of my knowledge.

_____
Signature of imposter

_____
Date

Knowingly submitting false information on this affidavit could subject you to criminal prosecution for perjury. Have this form notarized; the imposter should pay this cost.

Form Letter 3

I, _____

(name of imposter), admit that I made charges in the name of

_____

(name of victim) in the amount of _____
(insert dollar amount).

I hereby agree to repay this debt in the following way:
    The total amount I will repay is:_____

    I agree to make monthly payments of _____
    by the 15th of each month for a total of _____ months to

_____

    (Creditor at specific address).

I will provide the following collateral to the victim until payment in full is made:

_____

    (If it is possible to get a few valuables to secure payment that would provide motivation.)

I acknowledge that this debt will be transferred to my name and I will indemnify the victim for any payments or out of pocket costs he/she has made as a result of this use of his/her credit.

I assume full responsibility for this debt and will sign a letter asking the creditor to transfer this account to name, Social Security number and address and that this account be reflected on my credit profile with the major credit reporting agencies.

I hereby agree to enter into emotional counseling or a mental health program, _____ (name of program), for _____ (how often, how long).

    (Options include but are not limited to: AA, residential substance abuse programs, gamblers anonymous, private therapy.)

I hereby agree that I will provide _____
(name of victim) proof of my attendance of program listed
above. (AA and other programs have forms that get signed each
time they attend.)

I hereby acknowledge that this is a legally binding agreement
that is enforceable in a court of law and know that any breach
of this agreement is subject to the laws of this state.

_____
Signature of victim

_____
Date

I declare under penalty of perjury that this declaration is true
and correct to the best of my knowledge.

_____
Signature of victim

_____
Date

**Knowingly submitting false information on this affidavit could
subject you to criminal prosecution for perjury. Have this form
notarized; the imposter should pay this cost.**

Contact ITRC at *www.idtheftcenter.org* or *www.identitytheft.org* for current information. A variety of regularly updated fact sheets on identity theft are available.

Afterword

Like living with the ongoing threat of terrorism, one of the keys to dealing with identity theft is to find that delicate balance between reasonable caution and getting on with your life. On one hand, there is no simple way to completely eliminate the crime of identity theft in our society. On the other hand, as we've clearly seen, there *are* quite a few things you can start doing...today...that will minimize your risk.

We can't and shouldn't live in fear, mistrusting every individual and organization with whom we come in contact. But also we can't allow ourselves to become helpless victims of corrupt individuals and organizations.

The identity theft problem is one that will neither be solved easily or quickly, nor will it be solved by one book, one person, or one organization. The solution will only come through mutual effort, education, and intelligent discourse.

I will end on a confessional note: Carson James is not real. Neither are Jane, Cat Girl, Oscar, or Felix (except in the hearts of "Odd Couple" devotees). I created them to get your attention, though I suspect that the real stories in Chapter 3 made my fabricated ones pale by comparison.

Appendix A

An Excerpt From:

Human Identification Theory and the Identity Theft Problem

by Lynn M. LoPucki, University of California, Los Angeles—School of Law.

Reprinted with permission. Originally published in *Texas Law Review*, Vol. 80, February 2002

Author's note: With the exception of bold-faced subheads included purely for organizational purposes, all text is a direct quote from the above paper unless otherwise noted. Individual paragraphs have been reorganized to more clearly "flow" in this shortened version of what was originally a 53-page manuscript.

Why the current system can't solve the identity-theft problem

...People impersonate others for a wide variety of purposes. Spies impersonate people entitled to the information the spies seek. Persons who are arrested often claim to be someone else so they will receive the benefit of that person's previously clean record and avoid soiling their own. A student may impersonate another student who has the academic record necessary to be admitted to the institution the impersonator would like to attend; a job applicant may impersonate some specific person who had the credentials required for the job the applicant seeks. The vast bulk of identity theft, however, occurs in the consumer credit system. Thieves impersonate persons with good credit so they can borrow money

...Although the impersonated victim is not involved in (any) fraudulent credit transactions perpetrated by the identity thief and (may suffer little if any) direct loss from them, the impersonated victim usually suffers from their secondary effects. Thinking that it extended credit to the impersonated victim, the defrauded creditor initiates collection action...(which) may include phone calls, written demands for payment, refusal to extend future credit, legal action and, perhaps most importantly, credit reporting.

Identity theft is possible under the current system because the impersonation takes place in private, entirely isolated from the victim's web of personal relationships. The imposter applies for credit from someone who does not know the victim—someone who must identify the applicant solely by matching personal characteristics to data. The current system has no means of reaching back to a person's web of relationships for identification until the imposter has defaulted and the victim has been damaged by a false credit report.

In the current system, human identification proceeds outside the control of the persons whose credit records are at risk. Even consumers who know they are under attack have no way to take control of the process. Because the identification process currently is entirely private, identity thieves are able to ply their trade without ever exposing themselves to serious risk of arrest and prosecution. With the exponential growth of identity theft in recent years, there is a growing recognition that changes must be made. The proposed system would make key portions of the process of identification public and make it possible for participants to control that process—without compromising participant's privacy.

The problem is not that thieves have access to personal information, but that creditors and credit reporting agencies often lack both the means and the incentives to correctly identify the persons on whom they report. The proposed solution set forth below...(describes) a physical system that would make it possible for consumers to control the process of their own identification. The system would be voluntary for all participants, but creditors and credit reporting agencies who chose to identify and report on consumers without following the consumers' instructions would be liable for any resulting misidentifications.

Proposals currently before Congress to prevent identity theft by attempting to make social security numbers and mother's maiden names private would not work...Information that has essentially been public for decades cannot be made private by passing a law against selling it. For one thing, that law could apply and be enforced only within the United States. Trading in social security numbers would continue offshore. The social security numbers and mother's maiden names of Americans living today will never be secure.

Proposals that would bar the use of social security numbers in human identification almost invariably fail to address the obvious systems concerns. If social security numbers cannot be used in matching, what will be? If the answer is that matching will not take place, how will society prevent fraud by those who apply for credit, public benefits, driver's licenses, employment, and numerous other privileges that today are granted based on one's past record or other status?

Whatever objections one may have to the proposed system must be evaluated in light of the alternatives. The current system for dealing with identity theft is failing. It relies on the quixotic hope that with sufficient effort consumers can keep their names, social security numbers, and mother's maiden names secret.

The most important reason for adopting the system proposed here is to give relief to the hundreds of thousands of Americans who have been and will be victims of identity theft. Absent such a system, the victims of identity theft will remain in a Kafkaesque nightmare in which no sure means exist for claiming their own identities.

An overview of the proposed system

Most people live their lives in some sort of community. Within that community, numerous relatives, friends, and acquaintances can link their appearance to their name and know how to contact them. That web of relationships is easily linked to less public identifying characteristics such as social security number and mother's maiden name. Within that web, impersonation would be impossible.

The proposed system would give persons concerned about identity theft the option to publicly register their identities and publicly provide information for contacting and identifying them. By consulting the web site and following the instructions posted on it, extenders of consumer credit could quickly and accurately determine if an applicant for credit on a participant's account was an imposter. The creditors would have two incentives to consult the web site: lower credit losses and continuation of the current exemption the creditors enjoy against liability for false reporting on the victims of identity theft.

The (proposed system) would have no detrimental effect on privacy, even for those who participate. Those participants will make public their social security numbers, but those numbers reveal nothing significant about them. Governments and businesses have in the past been all too willing to give personal information to anyone who knows the person's social security number and is willing to impersonate. The proposed system would end those practices by making clear that knowledge of someone's social security number is not a reasonable basis for thinking the knower is that person. Most participants will publicly list contact information, but that information need not be in any way personal. Most importantly, no person would be required or even pressured to participate—except for the pressure exerted by the growing presence of identity theft.

The proposed system would enable a creditor who seeks to determine the identity of a credit applicant to contact the true owner of that identity for confirmation...

Participation in the proposed system would be optional for consumers. Probably most would not participate. Participation would not be de facto compulsory because the only incentive offered to participants would be the direct benefits from participation—control over the process of their own identification. Participation would also be optional for creditors. Creditors that choose accept a credit applicant's assertion of identity without checking the system would lose their statutory exemption from liability for false reporting with respect to that identification. Alternatively, creditors could avoid the effects of the system by declining to lend to some, or all, participating consumers.

The proposed system has the capacity to reach the web during the primary identification process—before any damage has been done. The first opportunity would be during the agency's investigation of an account claimant...The capacity and opportunity to do the investigations, combined with the necessity for the imposter to appear personally without knowing what investigation had been done, would render the system impenetrable to identity thieves.

The proposed system could also reach into the true owner's web of personal relationships in deciding challenges to a person's right to control an account. The existence of the web assures that if an investigation proceeds far enough, the imposter will be discovered...

How the system would work

1. Primary Identification

...Participation in the proposed system would be limited to persons who own social security accounts. A person who wished to participate, but was not eligible for lack of an account, could open one by applying to the Social Security Administration for a social security number. An account owner who wished to participate in the proposed system would begin by filing a claim of ownership of the account with the government agency designated to administer the proposed system. The claimant would initiate the primary identification process by essentially the same procedure currently used to obtain a replacement social security card. That is, the claimant would furnish a copy of a document acceptable to the agency for identification—such as a driver's license or a passport—by mail to the designated agency. The information supplied would include only information already in the possession of the Social Security Administration—the social security account number, the date and place of birth of the owner of the account, and the names of the owner's parents. The law would continue to prohibit false claims to ownership of a social security account and provide criminal penalties.

If the claimant's name did not match the name on the social security account, the claim would be denied and the claimant advised to contact the Social Security Administration to correct the record. When the claimant's name matched the name of the account owner on the records of the Social Security Administration, the designated agency would list the claimant's name and Social security number on the web site and commence an investigation to confirm that the claimant is the owner of the account.

The investigation would in most cases be perfunctory. First, the investigator would confirm the issuance of the document submitted for identification with the organization that issued it and match the claimant's characteristics as listed on the document copy with the claimant's characteristics as listed on the records of the issuer. In most cases, that would mean calling the Department of Motor Vehicles to confirm that the driver's license presented as identification was genuine and unaltered. Second, the investigator would purchase a "credit header" from a credit reporting agency for the social security number claimed. By matching the characteristics on the header—name, social security number, telephone number, and perhaps mother's maiden name—with the characteristics furnished by the claimant to the designated agency, the investigator could determine whether the identity proposed for the web site under that social security number was consistent with the identity used with the number in credit reporting.

In cases involving suspicious circumstances, the investigation would be more extensive...

To complete the process, the claimant would be required to appear personally at an office of the designated agency and sign a statement under penalty of perjury supporting his or her claim of identity. If the results of the investigation were consistent with the claim, the applicant would take control of the account at the time of the personal appearance by furnishing identification or contact information for posting on the web site. For example, the applicant might furnish identification by having the agency take a photograph during that personal appearance or furnish contact information in the form of an email address or telephone number. If the investigation discovered the claim to be bogus, the false claimant could be arrested during the appearance. If the investigation prior to the appearance were inconclusive, the investigator could interview the claimant at the time of the appearance.

2. The Web Site

The designated agency would maintain a database containing the identification and contact information furnished, and display the information from that data base on a web site. Read-only access to the web site would be unrestricted.

As previously noted, when an applicant claimed ownership of a social security account, notice of the claim would be immediately listed on the web site. Once the designated agency determined that the claimant was the true owner of the account, the designated agency would note its determination on the web site as well.

The owner could then add any of three types of information to his or her record to be displayed on the web site. First, each owner would be strongly urged to list contact information in the form of a mailing address, a telephone number, an email address, or a fax number. Participants who wish to receive encrypted email, could display their public keys, but use of the public keys would be mandatory only for creditors already making general use of encrypted email. The contact could be directly with the owner or through the owner's trusted intermediary. Listings would not state which.

Second, the owner could list the owner's biometric identifying characteristics. They might include height, weight, year of birth, gender, hair color, eye color, race, a photograph, fingerprints, or even DNA sequences.

Third, the owner could choose one of several standard instructions to potential creditors for identifying a person purporting to be the owner. Possible instructions would be:

a. Identifications require personal appearance and the matching of personal characteristics to the displayed biometric identifying characteristics.

b. Identifications may proceed on notice to the owner through at least one of the contact channels listed.

c. Identifications may proceed on notice to the owner through at least two of the contact channels listed. If both new and old contact information is listed, one of the two channels listed must be old and the other new.

d. Identifications may proceed only on notice to, and confirmation of receipt by, the account owner.

When the use of public key encryption becomes sufficiently common, identification based on receipt of, and response to, encrypted email should become an additional option.

An owner could change the information on the web site by sending an instruction to the designated agency. Before making the change, the designated agency would identify the sender by the method indicated on the web site. Ordinarily, that would require the agency to notify the account owner of the request. Changed contact information would be marked obsolete but would remain on the web site for a reasonable period of time after the change, probably sixty to ninety days.

After an owner had assumed control of his or her account, the owner might inadvertently lose that control. This would occur, for example, if an owner required notice by telephone and confirmation of receipt, but the owner had surrendered the telephone number. In such a case, the owner would have to be re-identified by the primary identification process.

...The data base and web site could both be fully scalable for use with 100 participants or 100 million participants...

3. Secondary Identification

To use the system, the person to whom a credit application is made obtains the applicant's name and social security number from the applicant and then checks the web site to determine if the account claimed is that of a system participant. If not, the creditor proceeds just as it does in the current system. If the account claimed is that of a system participant, the creditor follows the web site instructions for making the identification. In most cases, those instructions will require that the creditor telephone the account owner or mail a notice to the account owner. But participants who wish to do so may require contact by email, including encrypted email if the particular creditor uses it generally. If the applicant is the account owner, the applicant will confirm his or her own identity in response to the contact. If the applicant is not the owner, the owner will so advise the creditor and the creditor will decline credit.

4. The Process for Challenging Agency Determinations

At any given time, the web site would show the identity of the person recognized as the account owner by the designated agency. Any person claiming to be the rightful owner could file a written challenge to the agency's determination that someone else was the owner. Upon receipt of the challenge, the agency would immediately note its making on the web site, notify the person currently recognized as the account owner using the old contact information on the web site, and commence an investigation. In most cases, the investigator would be able to resolve the challenge quickly and easily. Seldom could two persons each make a plausible claim to the same social security number. If not definitively resolved sooner, the investigation would end in a hearing at which both claimants would be required to appear.

Eventually, identity thieves would attempt to infiltrate the system, by stealing operating manuals or corrupting employees. But the public nature of the system would make it virtually impervious to such efforts. Every incident in which an imposter obtained control of an account—for even the briefest period— would be a matter of public record on the web site. If the site also indicated the name and office of the investigator for every participant, internal auditors and members of the public could quickly and easily identify the weaknesses in the system and insist on their correction.

The proposed system would not need to catch every imposter who attempted to take control of an account to render takeover attempts not cost effective. It would need to catch only a large enough percentage of them that the risk of attempting to take control of someone else's account would clearly outweigh the benefit of taking control.

Changes in the law necessary to implement this new system

...First, creditors who do not check the web site and follow a consumer's instructions should not be entitled to the statutory exemption from liability contained in the Fair Credit Reporting Act. If such a creditor extends credit to an imposter and then falsely reports the extension as having been to the consumer, the creditor should be liable to the consumer for damages.

Second, because participants' social security numbers would be displayed publicly, those numbers should no longer be used as passwords. Federal law should recognize their new status with a declaration that a person's knowledge of a number displayed on the web site is not evidence that the person is the owner of the corresponding social security account. Consumers who chose not to participate in the proposed system could continue their efforts to keep their social security numbers private and creditors, credit reporting agencies, and others could continue to use them as passwords to the extent permitted under current law.

Third, federal law should bar use of information obtained from the web site for marketing purposes. The restrictions would be backed by civil and criminal penalties for violation. The designated agency would have enforcement responsibility and private actions seeking statutory damages would also be permitted. Federal law should bar creditors from using caller ID blocking devices when calling system participants to confirm their identities.

Appendix B

Testimony of John D. Woodward, Jr., Attorney-at-Law

For the Hearing of the Subcommittee on Domestic and
International Monetary Policy,
Committee on Banking and Financial Services,
U.S. House of Representatives
One Hundred Fifth Congress
On "Biometrics and the Future of Money"
May 20, 1998

...From activities as diverse as the elaborate security of the Winter Olympics in Nagano, Japan to the daily operations of the Purdue Employees Federal Credit Union in the Hoosier State, both the public and private sectors are making extensive use of biometrics. This new technological reality relies on "the body as password" for human recognition purposes to provide better security, increased efficiency and improved service. As the technology becomes more economically viable, technically perfected and widely deployed, biometrics will become the passwords and personal identification numbers (PINs) of the twenty-first century. In the process, biometrics could refocus the way Americans look at the brave new world of personal information.

Information privacy concerns related to private sector use of biometrics can be effectively accommodated by a federally-mandated biometric blueprint based on a Code of Fair Information Practices (CFIP). In essence, such a biometric blueprint would require that an individual have notice of and give consent to the use of his biometric identification information. Moreover, organizations using biometric identification information would be required by law to safeguard their databases and to permit the individual to correct any mistakes in the data collected.

...Three important points need to be stressed...:

1. Biometrics should not be construed as privacy's foe. Quite to the contrary, biometrics is privacy's friend. Biometrics is privacy's friend because biometrics:

    *   Safeguards information integrity and thwarts identity theft;

    *   Limits access to sensitive information; and,

    *   Serves as a privacy enhancing technology.

2. A pro-privacy position should not be construed as an anti-biometric stance: You can be a friend of privacy and a friend of biometrics. Moreover, limited government regulation of private sector use of this technology is not opposing biometrics but rather promoting biometrics. Appropriate policymaking can greatly increase public acceptance of this technology.

3. The law and policy concerns of biometrics cannot be left solely to politicians, lawyers and advocates.

Examination of the Legal Status Quo

...In the American legal experience, privacy protections have followed two basic pathways depending on whether the source of the privacy intrusion is a governmental or private sector activity. While privacy is not explicitly cited in the text, the Constitution, through the Bill of Rights, protects the individual from government's intrusion into the individual's privacy. For example, the Bill of Rights contains privacy protections in the First Amendment rights of freedom of speech, press and association; the Third Amendment prohibition against the quartering of soldier's in one's home; the Fourth Amendment right to be free from unreasonable searches and seizures; the Fifth Amendment right against self-incrimination; and the Ninth Amendment's provision that "[t]he enumeration in the Constitution, of certain rights, shall not be construed to deny or disparage others retained by the people;" and the Tenth Amendment's provision that "[t]he powers not delegated to the United States by the Constitution, nor prohibited by it to the States, are reserved to the States respectively, or to the people."

With respect to private sector actions, the Constitution traditionally embodies what is essentially a laissez-faire spirit. As constitutional law scholar Laurence Tribe has noted, "[T]he Constitution, with the sole exception of the Thirteenth Amendment prohibiting slavery, regulates action by the government rather than the conduct of private individuals and groups." With respect to the conduct of private individuals, the Supreme Court has been reluctant to find a privacy right in personal information given voluntarily by an individual to private parties.[3]

...For private sector intrusions into privacy, the common-law, through its doctrines of contract, tort and property, has, in varying degrees, attempted to provide certain protections for the individual. However, the law has not used these doctrines to protect individual information in private sector databases. Generally, as a matter of law, an individual in possession of information has the right to disclose it.

Accordingly, the private sector enjoys great leeway as far as what it can do with an individual's information. As two privacy scholars have concluded: "Except in isolated categories of data, an individual has nothing to say about the use of information that he has given about himself or that has been collected about him. In particular, an organization can acquire information for one purpose and use it for another...generally the private sector is not legislatively-constrained."[4]

Examination of the Policy Status Quo

At present, Congress and the state legislatures have left biometrics essentially unregulated from the standpoint of individual privacy protections related to private sector use. However, Congress and several state legislatures have mandated the use of biometric scanning for certain public sector applications...

...Despite these forays into the world of biometric applications, Congress and the state legislatures have taken precious few steps to regulate biometrics related to privacy concerns stemming from private sector use...

The federal government's executive branch has taken impressive initiatives with respect to biometric research and applications... However, to date, the executive branch has not attempted any wide-ranging regulation of biometric activities in the private sector. While the Department of Commerce and Federal Trade Commission (FTC), for example, have shown concern for various privacy issues, they have not yet delved into the biometric arena.

Biometrics as Privacy's Friend

...While critics of biometrics contend that this new technology is privacy's foe, the opposite is, in fact, true. Biometrics is a friend of privacy whether used in the private or public sectors. Biometrics proves itself as privacy's friend when it is deployed as a security safeguard to prevent identity theft and fraud.

To consider a specific example drawn from the financial services industry but applicable to almost any fraud prevention scenario, criminals eagerly exploit weaknesses with the present access systems, which tend to be based on passwords and PINs, by clandestinely obtaining these codes. They then surreptitiously access a legitimate customer's account. The honest client effectively loses control over her personal account information. Her financial integrity is compromised and her finances are gone because a criminal has gained unauthorized access to the information. In effect, she has suffered an invasion of her privacy related to her financial integrity. With biometric-based systems, identity theft, while never completely defeated, becomes more difficult for the criminal element to perpetrate. The use of biometrics means less identity theft and less consumer fraud which means greater protection of consumers' financial integrity. Numerous examples exist of impostors masquerading under false identity which biometrics could prevent...

Biometrics becomes a staunch friend of privacy when the technology is used for access control purposes, thereby restricting unauthorized personnel from gaining access to sensitive personal information. For example, biometrics can be effectively used to limit access to a patient's medical information stored on a computer database. Instead of relying on easily compromised passwords and PINs, a biometric identifier is required at a computer workstation to determine database access. The same biometric systems can be used for almost any information database (including databases containing biometric identifiers) to restrict or compartment information based on the "Need to Know" principle.

Biometrics also protects information privacy to the extent that biometrics can be used, through the use of a biometric log-on explained above, to keep a precise record of who accesses what personal information within a computer network. For example, individual tax records would be much better protected if an Internal Revenue Service official had to use her biometric identifier to access them, knowing that an audit trail was kept detailing who accessed which records. Far less snooping by curious bureaucrats would result.

In addition to safeguarding information integrity and limiting access to sensitive information, biometrics can also enhance privacy in broader ways. For example, biometrics can be used to control access to information, such as financial records, without requiring specific identification of the person accessing the information. In this way, privacy is enhanced by ensuring that only authorized persons can access the information, but obviating the need to specifically identify those individuals who have accessed the information..

The applications of this type of anonymous verification system are extensive. Most notably, such a biometric-based system would seem to provide a ready commercial encryption capability. Moreover, rather than technological advances eroding individual privacy expectations as has transpired, for example, with the Environmental Protection Agency's use of a special aerial surveillance camera to photograph private property,[10] biometrics, as used to create an anonymous encryption system, would provide for privacy enhancement.

...[M]any of the criticisms of biometrics are off the mark in that they should really be aimed at the exploitation of contemporary information systems which are the result of America's economic, political and technological changes. Moreover, the criticisms fail to acknowledge that in many situations knowing an individual's identity is necessary and prudent.[11]

The Need For a Biometric Blueprint

In balancing the privacy concerns with the benefits biometrics provides in private sector applications, several options exist for our nation's policymakers. To summarize, these options include:

1. Laissez-faire Approach, i.e. "If it ain't broke, don't fix it";

2. Self Regulatory Approach, based on voluntary industry codes;

3. Government Regulatory Approach, at the state or federal level; or

4. Hybrid Approach, featuring a combination of the above.

... Congress should encourage biometric applications by mandating the adoption of a biometric blueprint based on a Code of Fair Information Practices (CFIP). The federal government should promote biometrics by requiring the private sector to adhere to a sensible CFIP-based biometric blueprint.

The adoption of a biometric blueprint at the federal level is an effective way to balance privacy concerns with the benefits of biometrics. We are well aware of problems of identity theft and consumer fraud resulting from the compromise of traditional forms of personal identification such as names, addresses, social security numbers and driver's license numbers. Moreover, just like an individual who gives personal information in other non-biometric contexts, the individual providing biometric identification information to an organization can similarly expect that his information will be used for the specific purpose for which he gave it and in his best interest, not in any way to his detriment. The individual does not expect to be annoyed, pressured, harassed or harmed by its use.

As a bedrock premise, a CFIP establishes rights for data subjects and places responsibilities on the data collectors. In this sense, it provides for the mutuality of control of the information provided. The CFIP-based Congressional biometric blueprint should consist of five basic principles which include:

1. Notice: The clandestine capture of biometric identification information in the private sector would be strictly prohibited. No secret databases should exist.

2. Access: The individual (or data subject) has the right to access his information in the database. Specifically, the individual must be able to find out if his biometric identification information is in the database and

how it is being used by the data collector. Accordingly, the data collector would be required to disclose its privacy practices.

3. Correction Mechanism: The individual must be able to correct or make changes to any biometric identification information in the database. As one of the technical advantages of biometrics is that they are based on physical characteristics or personal traits which rarely change over time, this principle would likely not be called into play too often.

4. Informed Consent: Before any information can be disclosed to third parties, the individual must consent. The individual must voluntarily and knowingly provide his biometric identification information to the data collector in the primary market. Once in the possession of the data collector, this information would then be governed by a use limitation principle. This means that the individual has consented that the information she provided would be used in the primary market for a purpose defined by the data collector and known to the individual. The individual must knowingly consent to any exchange, such as buying and selling of his biometric identification information, before it could be traded in a secondary market. Reasonable exceptions can be accommodated as appropriate for academic research and law enforcement, for example.

5. Reliability & Safeguarding: The organization responsible for the database must guarantee the reliability of the data and safeguard the information. Any data collector that collects and stores biometric identification information must guarantee the reliability of the data for its intended use and must take precautions to safeguard the data. At its most basic level, appropriate managerial and technical controls must

be used to protect the confidentiality and integrity of the information. The controls would include making the database and the computer system physically secure. Data collectors should explore the option of encrypting the biometric data to help further safeguard the information from disclosure.

Conclusion

...We are now eyeball to eyeball with a new, exciting technology that can be used in robust ways by the public and private sectors. A biometric blueprint can be used to make this new technology even more acceptable and beneficial for private sector use, particularly in the banking and financial services industry. It is surely better to have a far-sighted biometric policy that deals with the face of a new technological reality now than to point fingers of blame later.

Biographical information

John D. Woodward, Jr., an attorney, lectures and writes regularly on the law and policy concerns of biometrics. He has authored numerous articles on biometrics which have been published in *University of Pittsburgh Law Review, Proceedings of the IEEE, American Banker, Biometric Technology Today, Information Security, Legal Times,* CTST '98 Proceedings, CTST '97 Proceedings, and CTST '96 (Government) Proceedings.

Mr. Woodward has written articles on other legal and professional topics which have appeared in numerous publications. Before practicing law, he served as an Operations Officer for the Central Intelligence Agency for 12 years. In his last assignment, he was the CIA Staff Assistant to the Under Secretary of Defense for Policy at the Pentagon. Mr. Woodward's overseas assignments included tours in East Asia and Africa. He speaks Japanese and Thai.

Notes

Author's Note: Due to the abridgement of Mr. Woodward's testimony, footnoted material may have been eliminated from the text.

[1] I gratefully acknowledge the assistance of Arthur S. DiDio, M.D., J.D., and Professor Steven Goldberg of Georgetown University Law Center who kindly reviewed this testimony and contributed comments. Biographical information about the witness is included at Appendix I.

[2] Charles Fried, AN ANATOMY OF VALUES, 140 (1970); Richard B. Parker, A Definition of Privacy, 27 RUT. L. REV. 275, 281 (1974);Tom Gerety, Redefining Privacy, 12 HARV. C.R.-C.L. L. REV. 233, 236 (1977); United States v. Westinghouse Elec. Corp., 638 F. 2d 570, 577 (3rd Cir. 1980)(holding that medical records of a private sector employee, while within the ambit of constitutional privacy protection, could nonetheless be disclosed to a government agency upon a proper showing of governmental interest). See also Fred H. Cate, Privacy in the Information Age 19-31 (1997).

[3] See Smith v. Maryland, 442 U.S. 735 (1979); United States v. Miller, 425 U.S. 435 (1976).

[4] MARC ROTENBERG & EMILIO CIVIDANES, THE LAW OF INFORMATION PRIVACY: CASES & COMMENTARY 22 (1997).

[5] The Truck and Bus Safety and Regulatory Reform Act of 1988, Pub. L. No. 100-690, Section 9105(a), 102 Stat. 4530 (1988), (codified as amended at 49 U.S.C. Section 31309(d)(2) (1994)).

[6] The Immigration and Nationality Act (as amended). See also 8 U.S.C.A. Section 1101(a)(6) (West Supp. 1997).

[7] See Brian J. Wing, New York State Department of Social Services: Automated Finger Imaging, (March 1997) at 677-684, in CTST '97 CONFERENCE PROCEEDINGS (1997)(explaining how "New York State has implemented the nation's first statewide automated finger imaging system (AFIS) for the identification of public assistance recipients."); David Mintie, Biometrics for State Identification Systems—Operational Experiences, in CTST '98 CONFERENCE PROCEEDINGS (1998).

[8] See State ex rel. Beacon Journal Publishing Co. v. Akron, 70 Ohio Sr. 3d 605 (1994).

[9] See, e.g., Ann Cavoukian, Privacy and Biometrics: An Oxymoron or Time to take a Second Look? presented at Computers, Freedom and Privacy '98 (1998).

[10] See Dow Chemical Co. v. United States, 476 U.S. 227 (1985)(holding that Dow had no reasonable, legitimate and objective expectation of privacy in the area photographed); see also United States v. Knotts, 460 U.S. 276 (1983).

[11] For a discussion of the criticisms of biometrics, see, e.g., John D. Woodward, Biometrics: Privacy's Foe or Privacy's Friend?, 85 Proceedings of the IEEE 1480 (1997). For a discussion of the concerns raised by government-mandated use of biometrics, see, e.g., John D. Woodward, Biometric Scanning, Law & Policy: Identifying the Concerns; Drafting the Biometric Blueprint, 59 U. Pitt. L. Rev. 97 (1997).

[12] United States General Accounting Office, Electronic Benefits Transfer: Use of Biometrics to Deter Fraud in the Nationwide EBT Program, GAO/OSI-95-20, Sept. 1995 (prepared at the request of Representative Kenneth E. Bentsen, Jr.).

[13] See "People Patterns: Fingerprints? No Problem," Wall Street Journal, Jan. 31, 1997.

[14] See, e.g., Whalen v. Roe, 429 U.S. 589, 593-595 (1977) (but note that in Whalen, these criminal sanctions applied to unauthorized disclosure from a government-mandated database containing the names and addresses of patients receiving certain prescription drugs).

Appendix

C

FTC Response

Prepared Statement of the
Federal Trade Commission on Identity Theft:
the FTC'S Response Before the Subcommittee on
Technology, Terrorism and Government Information of
the Senate Judiciary Committee
Washington, D.C.
March 20, 2002

I. Introduction

Madam Chairman, and members of the Committee, I am Howard Beales, Director of the Bureau of Consumer Protection, Federal Trade Commission ("FTC" or "Commission"). I appreciate the opportunity to present the Commission's views on one of the most serious consequences that can result from the misuse of consumers' personal information: identity theft.[1]

The passage of the Identity Theft and Assumption Deterrence Act of 1998 ("Identity Theft Act")[2] brought identity theft to the forefront of the public's attention. Media attention and high profile cases[3] have heightened concerns about the serious injury caused by identity theft.

In particular, the specter of identity theft has focused consumers' concern about the misuse of their personally identifying information. There is good reason for this concern. Identity theft can result in temporary and sometimes permanent financial loss when wages are garnished, tax refunds are withheld, or liens are placed on victims' property as a result of someone else's criminal use of their identity. Beyond direct financial loss, consumers report being denied employment, credit, loans (including mortgages and student loans), government benefits, utility and telecommunications services, and apartment leases when credit reports and background checks are littered with the fraudulently incurred debts or wrongful criminal records of an identity thief.

The 1998 legislation positioned the FTC to play a key role in the national dialogue on identity theft. The FTC enforces a number of laws that address consumers' privacy,[4] and intends to increase substantially the resources devoted to privacy protection. The FTC's identity theft program is an important part of that initiative. Consumer and victim assistance, data sharing with law enforcement and financial institutions, and cooperative efforts with the private sector are among the most visible examples of the FTC's efforts.[5] Recent FTC initiatives, including a Spanish language version of our consumer brochure, law enforcement training, and a standard Identity Theft Affidavit, complement the measures we have already undertaken to fulfill our mandate under the 1998 Act.

II. The FTC's Response to the Identity Theft Act

The Identity Theft Act directed the Commission to establish procedures to: log the receipt of complaints by victims of identity theft; provide identity theft victims with informational materials; and refer complaints to appropriate entities, including the major national consumer reporting agencies and law enforcement agencies.[6] To fulfill the purposes of the Act, the Commission implemented a plan with three principal components: a toll-free telephone hotline, a database of identity theft complaints, and consumer and business education.

(1) Toll Free Hotline. The Commission established its toll-free telephone number (the "hotline"), 1-877-ID-THEFT (438-4338) in November 1999. The hotline now responds to an average of over 3000 calls per week. When consumers call to report identity theft, the hotline counselors enter information from their complaints into the Identity Theft Data Clearinghouse (the "Clearinghouse") —a centralized database used to aid law enforcement and track trends involving identity theft.

The counselors advise the callers to contact the credit reporting agencies and the entities where the fraudulent accounts were opened in order to place a fraud alert on their credit files and shut down the fraudulent accounts, respectively. They also encourage consumers to contact their local police departments to file a police report, both because local law enforcement may be in the best position to catch and prosecute identity thieves and because a police report helps consumers demonstrate to creditors and debt collectors that they are in fact genuine victims of identity theft. Forty-seven states have enacted their own identity theft laws and the FTC hotline phone counselors, in appropriate circumstances, will refer consumers to other state and local authorities. Lastly, when another federal agency has a program in place to assist consumers, callers are referred to that agency.[7]

Of the callers to our hotline, thirty-four percent are seeking information about how to guard against identity theft.[8] The phone counselors provide suggestions on steps they should take to minimize their risk.

(2) Identity theft complaint database. The information that the consumers share with the phone counselors can

provide the foundation for investigation. The telephone counselors enter the complaints received by the FTC through the hotline, by mail, and through the FTC's secure on-line identity theft complaint form into the FTC's Clearinghouse database. In addition, the Social Security Administration's Office of Inspector General transfers into the Clearinghouse complaints of identity theft received by its consumer hotline.

The Clearinghouse is the federal government's centralized repository of consumer identity theft complaint information. It contains detailed information regarding the identity theft victim, the suspect, and the ways the identity thief misused the victim's personal information. More than 270 law enforcement agencies nationwide have signed confidentiality agreements that grant them membership and access to the Identity Theft Data Clearinghouse. The Clearinghouse information is available directly on members' desktop PCs via the FTC's secure law enforcement Web site, Consumer Sentinel. Access to the Clearinghouse information supports law enforcement agencies' efforts to combat identity theft by providing a range of complaints from which to augment their ongoing investigations and spot new patterns of illegal activity.

(3) Consumer and business education. The FTC has taken the lead in coordinating with other government agencies and organizations to develop and disseminate comprehensive consumer education materials for victims of identity theft and those concerned with preventing this crime. For example, in collaboration with other federal agencies, the FTC published a comprehensive informational booklet, Identity Theft: When Bad Things Happen to Your Good Name, in February 2000. Since its publication through February 2002, the FTC has distributed more than 600,000 hard copies of the booklet and recorded over 609,500 visits to our Web version. Other federal agencies have also printed and distributed this publication.

Consumers can also find comprehensive information about preventing and recovering from identify theft at the FTC's identity theft Web site, *www.consumer.gov/idtheft*. The site also links to a secure Web-based complaint form, allowing consumers to send complaints directly to the Clearinghouse. The FTC now receives an average of 400 complaints per week via the Internet; overall, more than 18,000 victims filed their identity theft complaints online as of the end of December 2001. The FTC's identity theft Web site had received more than 699,000 hits since it was launched in February 2000.

To expand the reach of our consumer education message, the FTC has begun an outreach effort to Spanish-speaking victims of identity theft. Just last month, we released a Spanish version of the Identity Theft booklet (Robo de Identidad: Algo malo puede pasarle a su buen nombre) and the ID Theft Affidavit (discussed below in Section III). In addition, we have added Spanish-speaking phone counselors to our hotline staff. We will soon launch a Spanish version of our online complaint form.

III. The FTC's Recent Collaborative and Outreach Efforts

Over the past year, the Commission has worked closely with other government agencies and private entities to encourage the investigation and prosecution of identity theft cases, and help consumers resolve identity theft problems.

(1) Law Enforcement. One of our goals is to provide support for identity theft prosecutions nationwide. In the past year, the Commission launched an identity theft case referral program in coordination with the United States Secret Service, which assigned a special agent on a full-time basis to the Commission to assist with identity theft issues.[9] The identity theft team, assisted by the special agent, develops case leads by examining significant patterns of identity theft activity in the database and by refining the data through the use of additional investigative resources.

Then, the team refers the case leads to one of the Financial Crimes Task Forces located throughout the country for further investigation and potential prosecution.

We provide support for law enforcement in other ways as well. Just last week, the FTC, in cooperation with the Department of Justice and the United States Secret Service, initiated a full day identity theft training seminar for state and local law enforcement officers. This first session was held in Washington, D.C.; subsequent sessions are planned in Chicago, Dallas, and San Francisco. The training seminar provides officers with technical skills and resources to enhance their efforts to combat identity theft, including strategies for both traditional and high-tech investigations. The training also identifies key components for successful actions by local, state, and federal prosecutors, and identifies resources, such as the Clearinghouse database, that are available to law enforcement when conducting identity theft investigations. Our goal is to encourage the prosecution of these cases at all levels of government.

(2) Private Industry. Identity theft victims spend significant time and effort restoring their good name and financial histories. Such burdens result, in part, from the need to complete a different fraud affidavit for each different creditor where the identity thief opened or used an account in their name.[10] To reduce that burden, the FTC worked to develop the ID Theft Affidavit ("Affidavit"). The Affidavit was the culmination of an effort we coordinated with private industry and consumer advocates to create a standard form for victims to use in absolving identity theft debts with each of the creditors where identity thieves opened accounts. The Affidavit is accepted by the three major credit reporting agencies and many creditors. From its release in August 2001 through February 2002, we have distributed more than 112,000 print copies of the Affidavit. There have also been nearly 185,000 hits to the Web version.

The FTC will continue working with private sector financial institutions to find additional ways to assist consumers. For example, we plan to work with businesses to highlight the importance of securing business records containing personally identifying information from would-be identity thieves, and providing consumers with notification in the event that their business records are compromised.

The FTC is examining other ways to lessen the difficulties and burdens faced by identity theft victims. One approach under consideration is to develop a joint "fraud alert initiative" with the three major credit reporting agencies ("CRAs"). This initiative would allow the FTC to transmit regularly to the three major CRAs requests from identity theft victims that fraud alerts be placed on their consumer report and copies of their reports be sent to them. This would eliminate the victim's need to contact each of the three major CRAs separately.

The CRAs have also asked the FTC to help promote their recent "police report initiative," which follows an earlier program supported by the FTC. After learning from our first twelve months of data that over 35% of victims contacting the FTC were not able to file police reports on identity theft, the FTC began working with the International Association of Chiefs of Police ("IACP") to encourage local police officers to write police reports for victims of identity theft. In November 2000, the IACP passed a Resolution in support of providing police reports to victims of identity theft and referring victims to the FTC's hotline.[11] In 2001, the consumers reporting to the FTC that the police would not issue a report dropped to 18%.[12] Under their new initiative, the CRAs have agreed to block inaccurate information resulting from the identity thief's activities from a victim's credit report if the victim provides the CRA with a police report on the incident. This program further speeds the process of rehabilitating the victim's good name.

IV. Identity Theft: How it Happens

Access to someone's personal information, through legal or illegal means, is the key to identity theft. Unlike most crimes where the victim is immediately aware of the assault, identity theft is often silent and invisible. Identity thieves do not need direct contact with their victims. All they need is access to some key components of a victim's personal information, which, for most Americans, may be maintained and used by numerous different public and private entities. Thus, it is hardly surprising that nearly 80% of the victims who report identity theft to the FTC do not know how or where the identity thief obtained their personal information.[13]

Some victims can recall an event or incident that they believe led to the identity theft. Eight percent of the victims who contacted the FTC had their wallet or purse lost or stolen. Three percent of the victims discovered that their mail had been stolen or that a fraudulent address change had been filed with a creditor. One percent of victims contacting the FTC recalled giving out personal information in response to a solicitation over the telephone or Internet, and another 1% reported that their identification had been stolen from their residence or car.[14]

Notably, 13% of the victims who contact the FTC report that they personally know the suspect. These relationships include family members (6%), other personal relationships, such as friends (3%), neighbors (2%), "significant others" or roommates (1%), or someone from the victim's workplace (1%).

The FTC also receives reports of identity theft from victims who learn of it only upon notification by their employer or an entity with whom they do business that their employee or customer records were stolen. This is called "business record identity theft." Between March 2000 through late December 2001, the Clearinghouse received reports regarding thirty-five different companies or institutions in which identity thieves stole records containing employees' or clients' personal information. The institutions included hospitals, tax preparers, municipalities and schools.[15] In many of these instances the records were stolen by insiders. Some of these thieves sold the records, while others exploited the information themselves. Some of the targeted companies sought our assistance in dealing with the aftermath of the theft, and in other cases, we reached out to them to offer assistance. When we provide assistance, we encourage the entities to contact the persons whose records were compromised, notify them that they were potential victims of identity theft, and advise them to contact the FTC's hotline.

While most victims do not know how or where the identity thief obtained their personal information, 68% of the complaints in the Clearinghouse do contain some identifying information about the suspect, such as a name, address, or phone number.[16] This includes any identifying information victims can provide about the suspect, which might be gleaned from the bills, letters or phones calls of would-be creditors and debt collectors, or from a victim's credit report. Such information about suspects allows law enforcement investigators to link seemingly unrelated complaints of identity theft to a common suspect.

V. Summary of Database Information

The Clearinghouse database has been in operation for more than two years.[17] For calendar year 2001, the Clearinghouse database contains over 86,000 complaints from ID theft victims. It also contains over 31,000 inquiries from consumers concerned about becoming victims of identity theft. These figures include contacts made directly to the FTC and data contributed by SSA-OIG.

While not comprehensive, information from the database can reveal information about the nature of identity theft activity. For example, the data show that California has the greatest overall number of victims in the FTC's database, followed by New York, Texas, Florida, and Illinois. On a per capita basis, per 100,000 citizens, the District of Columbia ranks first, followed by California, Nevada, Maryland and New York. The cities with the highest numbers of victims reporting to the database are New York, Chicago, Los Angeles, Houston and Miami.

Eighty-eight percent of victims reporting to the FTC provide their age.[18] The largest number of these victims (28%) were in their thirties. The next largest group includes consumers from age eighteen to twenty-nine (26%), followed by consumers in their forties (22%). Consumers in their fifties comprised 13%, and those age 60 and over comprised 9%, of the victims. Minors under 18 years of age comprised 2% of the victims.

As noted above, consumers often do not become aware of the crime for some time. Forty-four percent of victims who contact the FTC provide information on when the identity theft occurred and when they discovered it. The majority of these victims (69%) reported discovering the identity theft within 6 months of its first occurrence.[19] In fact, 44% noticed the identity theft within one month of its occurrence. However, 5% were unaware of the theft for longer than five years. On average, 12 months elapsed between the date the identity theft occurred and when the victim discovered it.

Thirty-five percent of the victims had not yet notified any credit bureau at the time they contacted the FTC;[20] 46% had not yet notified any of the financial institutions involved.[21] Fifty-four percent of the victims had not yet notified their local police department of the identity theft. By advising the callers to take these critical steps, we enable many victims to get through the recovery process more efficiently and effectively.

The Clearinghouse data, which represents complaints received by both the FTC and the SSA-OIG, also reveal how the thieves use the stolen identifying information. This data, summarized below, help provide a broad picture of the forms identity theft can take.[22]

♦ Credit Card Fraud: Forty-two percent of the victims in the Clearinghouse report credit card fraud. Sixty-two percent of these victims indicate that one or more new credit cards were opened in the victims' name. Twenty-four percent of these victims indicate that unauthorized charges were made on an existing credit card. Thirteen percent of the credit card fraud victims were not specific as to new or existing credit.

◆ Unauthorized Telecommunications or Utility Services: Twenty percent of the victims in the Clearinghouse report that the identity thief obtained unauthorized telecommunications or utility equipment or services in their name. New wireless telecommunications equipment and service comprised 48% of these complaints, new land line telephone service or equipment comprised 26%, new utilities such as electric or cable service comprised 12%, 11% of these complaints were not specific, and 2% comprised unauthorized charges to the victims' existing telecommunications or utility accounts.

◆ Bank Fraud: Thirteen percent of the victims report fraud on their demand deposit (checking or savings) accounts. Forty-seven percent of these victims report fraudulent checks written on their existing account, 20% report a new bank account opened in their name, 15% report unauthorized electronic withdrawals from their account, and 18% of these complaints were not specific.

◆ Employment: Nine percent of the victims in the database report that the identity thief used their personal information for employment purposes.

◆ Fraudulent Loans: Seven percent of the victims report that the identity thief obtained a loan in their name. Fifty-three percent of these complaints relate to a personal, student, or business loan, 28% concern auto loans or leases, 10% concern real estate loans, and 9% are unspecified.

◆ Government Documents or Benefits: Six percent of the victims report that the identity thief obtained government benefits or forged government documents in their name. Forty-four percent of these victims report a false driver's license, 11% report a false social security card, and 4% report the falsification of other government documents. Thirty-one percent report fraudulent claims for tax returns, 6% report fraudulent claims for government benefits, and 3% of these victims were not specific.

◆ Other Identity Theft: Nineteen percent of the victims in the database reported various other types of identity theft. Nine percent of these victims report that the thief assumed their identity to evade legal sanctions and criminal records (thus leaving the victim with a wrongful criminal or other legal record), 9% report that the thief obtained medical services, 6% report that the thief opened or accessed Internet accounts, 5% report that the thief leased a residence, 2% report that the thief declared bankruptcy in their name, 1% report that the thief purchased or traded in securities and investments, and 69% of these complaints were miscellaneous or unspecified.

◆ Multiple Types: Twenty percent of the victims in the database reported experiencing more than one of the above types of identity theft.

VI. Conclusion

Identity theft, once an unknown term, is now the subject of day time talk shows. The economic and non-economic injury caused by the misuse of consumers' personal information is significant. But there are real and positive steps we can take to alleviate the harm to consumers, and reduce the incidence of this crime. We are committed to working with our partners in the public and private sectors and will continue to forge a comprehensive approach to this challenge. I would be pleased to answer any questions you may have.

Endnotes

[1] The views expressed in this statement represent the views of the Commission. My oral presentation and responses to questions are my own and do not necessarily represent the views of the Commission or any Commissioner. The statistical information summarized in this statement covers the period of time from January 1 through December 31, 2001.

[2] Pub. L. No. 105-318, 112 Stat. 3010 (1998).

[3] Celebrities including Ted Turner, Martha Stewart and Oprah Winfrey have been reported in the press as being victims of identity theft. Jenny Lynn Bader, Paranoid Lately? You May Have Good Reason, N.Y. Times, March 25, 2001, at 4, Section 4.

[4] See, e.g., Federal Trade Commission Act, 15 U.S.C. § 41 et seq. (prohibiting deceptive or unfair acts or practices, including violations of stated privacy policies); Fair Credit Reporting Act, 15 U.S.C. § 1681 et seq. (addressing the accuracy, dissemination, and integrity of consumer reports); Telemarketing and Consumer Fraud and Abuse Prevention Act, 15 U.S.C. § 6101 et seq. (including the Telemarketing Sales Rule, 16 C.F.R. Part 310) (prohibiting telemarketers from calling at odd hours, engaging in harassing patterns of calls, and failing to disclose the identity of the seller and purpose of the call); Children's Online Privacy Protection Act, 15 U.S.C. § 6501 et seq. (prohibiting the collection of personally identifiable information from young children without their parents' consent); Identify Theft and Assumption Deterrence Act of 1998, 18 U.S.C. §1028 (directing the FTC to collect identity theft complaints, refer them to the appropriate credit bureaus and law enforcement agencies, and provide victim assistance); Gramm-Leach-Bliley Act, 15 U.S.C. § 6801 et seq. (requiring financial institutions to provide notices to consumers and allowing consumers (with some exceptions) to choose whether their financial institutions may share their information with third parties).

[5] Most identity theft cases are best addressed through criminal prosecution. The FTC itself has no direct criminal law enforcement authority.

[6] Pub. L. No. 105-318, 112 Stat. 3010 (1998) (Codified at 18 U.S.C. § 1028(a) note).

[7] For example, we may refer consumers to the Social Security Administration or their state department of motor vehicles.

[8] This statistic reflects the experience only of the consumers who contacted the FTC directly, and does not reflect data contributed by the Social Security Administration, Office of Inspector General ("SSA-OIG"). See infra at 4. While the SSA-OIG collects many of the same fields of data, they do not collect identical data. Unless otherwise noted, as in Section IV, the statistics used in this testimony include data from FTC and SSA-OIG.

[9] The referral program complements the regular use of the database by all law enforcers from their desk top computers.

[10] See ID Theft: When Bad Things Happen to Your Good Name: Hearing Before the Subcomm. on Technology, Terrorism and Government Information of the Senate Judiciary Comm. 106th Cong. (2000) (statement of Mrs. Maureen Mitchell, Identity Theft Victim).

[11] While this resolution is not binding, it sends an important message to the police around the country. The FTC has conveyed the same message in numerous law enforcement conferences across the country.

[12] Ninety-eight percent of victims reported whether they had been able to file a police report. The statistics regarding filing police reports reflect the experience only of the consumers who contacted the FTC directly, and do not reflect data contributed by the SSA-OIG, which does not collect such information. See supra at note 6.

[13] Nearly all of the statistics in Section IV reflect the experience only of the consumers who contacted the FTC directly, and do not reflect data contributed by the SSA-OIG. As indicated at note 6 supra, this is because the SSA-OIG data do not contain the same fields as the FTC data. Again, these statistics cover calendar year 2001.

[14] Recent Internet scams reportedly have emerged that try to trick consumers into revealing their information. For example, consumers report receiving emails from an entity purporting to be their Internet service provider, health insurer, or bank. The scammers request personal information, to confirm the

consumer's identity or eligibility for a program. In reality, these are traps for unwary consumers. We are looking for such scams and will take appropriate action.

[15] Jacob H. Fries, Worker Accused of Selling Colleagues' ID's Online, N.Y. Times, March 2, 2002, at B2.

[16] Suspect identifying information is collected both by FTC and SSA-OIG. This statistic includes data contributed by the SSA-OIG to the Clearinghouse.

[17] The Clearinghouse was established in November 1999. Because it is relatively new, the information in the database may be influenced by geographical differences in consumer awareness of the FTC's identity theft hotline and database.

[18] The statistics regarding consumers' age reflect the experience only of the consumers who contacted the FTC directly, and do not reflect data contributed by the SSA-OIG, which does not collect information about the victim's age. See supra at note 6.

[19] The statistics regarding when victims discover the crime and what entities they have notified reflect the experience only of the consumers who contacted the FTC directly, and do not reflect data contributed by the SSA-OIG, which does not collect such information. See supra at note 6.

[20] Ninety-five percent of victims reported whether they had contacted any credit bureaus.

[21] Sixty-three percent of victims reported whether they had notified any financial institutions.

[22] Many consumers experience more than one form of identity theft. Therefore, the percentages represent the number of consumers whose information was used for each various illegal purpose.

Appendix

Resources

Other Books by Robert Hammond

Repair Your Own Credit, Career Press, 3 Tice Road, P.O. Box 687, Franklin Lakes, NJ 07417, *www.careerpress.com*, 1 (800)CA-REER-1. Learn how to clear up negative credit on your reports and re-establish an excellent credit rating—regardless of your circumstances. This book is must reading for anyone who has ever had a problem with their credit history.

Life After Debt, Career Press. This book attacks the root causes of indebtedness and teaches consumers how to settle old accounts for pennies on the dollar. You'll learn how to stop collection-agency harassment, billing errors and discrimination. Contains sample letters for reducing monthly payments, credit reporting disputes and negotiated settlements.

Life Without Debt: Free Yourself from the Burden of Money Worries— Once and for All, Career Press. This companion to Life After Debt provides advanced strategies for surviving in this credit-oriented society. It reveals inside information about the credit system, from credit cards to home financing, student loans to cosigning for family members. It also contains special sections for dealing with the IRS, auto financing, bankruptcy and the psychology of debt and spending. Learn to save thousands of dollars on mortgages, auto loans and credit cards.

Other books

From Victim to Victor: A Step-by-Step Guide for Ending the Nightmare of Identity Theft, Mari J. Frank, Esq. and Dale Fetherling, Porpoise Press.

It's None of Your Business: A Complete Guide to Protecting Your Privacy, Identity & Assets, Larry Sontag, PMI Enterprises.

Identity Theft: The Cybercrime of the Millennium, John Q. Newman, Loompanics Unlimited.

The Guide to Identity Theft Prevention, Johnny R. May, 1st Books Library.

Newsletters

Consumer Affairs Letter
P.O. Box 65313
Washington, D.C. 20034
(202) 362-4279

Privacy Journal
P.O. Box 28577
Providence, RI 02908
(401) 274-7861

Privacy Newsletter
P.O. Box 8206
Philadelphia, PA 19101

Privacy Times
P.O. Box 21501
Washington, D.C. 20009
(202) 829-3660

Consumer Advocacy Organizations

CALPIRG (California Public Interest Research Group)
11965 Venice Blvd., Suite 408
Los Angeles, CA 90066
(213) 251-3680 x333
E-mail: calpirg@pirg.org
www.pirg.org/calpirg

Center for Democracy and Technology
1634 I Street NW, 11th Floor
Washington, D.C. 20096
(202) 637-9800
info@cdt.org
www.cdt.org

Center for Law in the Public Interest
10951 W. Pico Blvd., Third Floor
Los Angeles, CA 90064
(310) 470-3000

Computer Professionals for Social Responsibility
P.O. Box 717
Palo Alto, CA 94302
(650) 322-3778
cpsr@cpsr.org
www.cpsr.org

Consumer Action Credit and Finance Project
717 market Street Suite 310
San Francisco, Ca 94103
(415) 777-9635—complaint hot line
(415) 255-3879—publication orders
http://www.consumer-action.org

Consumer Federation of America
1424 16th St. NW, Suite 604
Washington, D.C. 20036
(202) 387-6121

Consumers Union
1666 Connecticut Ave. NW, Suite 310
Washington, D.C. 200009
(202) 461-6262

Electronic Privacy Information Center
666 Pennsylvania Ave., SE, Suite 301
Washington, D.C. 20003
(202) 483-1140
www.epic.org

The Foundation for Taxpayer and Consumer Rights
1750 Ocean Park Blvd., Suite 200
Santa Monica, CA 90405
(310) 392-0522
http://consumerwatchdog.org

Identity Theft Resource Center
Director, Linda Goldman-Foley
P.O. Box 26833
San Diego, CA 92196
(858) 693-7232
www.privacyrights.org

National Association of Attorneys General
Consumer Protection and Charities Counsel
750 First Street, N.W., Suite 1100
Washington, D.C. 20002
(202) 326-6000

National Center for Victims of Crime
2111 Wilson Blvd, Suite 300
Arlington, VA 22201
(800) FYI-CALL or (703) 276-2880
www.ncvc.org

National Consumer Law Center, Inc.
18 Tremont St., Suite 400
Boston, MA 02108
(617) 523-8010

National Fraud Information Center
Consumer Assistance Service
P.O. Box 65868
Washington, D.C. 20035
(800) 876-7060

National Organization for Victim Assistance (NOVA)
1757 Park Rd., NW
Washington, D.C. 20010
(202) 232-6682
(800) 879-6682 - hotline
http://access.digex.net/-nova

Office for Victims of Crime
633 Indiana Ave NW
Washington, D.C. 20531
(202) 727-0497

Privacy Rights Clearinghouse
Beth Givens, Director
1717 Kettner Avenue, Suite 105
San Diego, CA 92101
(619) 298-3396
www.privacyrights.org

PIRG (Public Interest Research Group)
Edmund Mierzwinski, Director
218 D St., SE
Washington D.C. 20003
(212) 546-9707
www.pirg.org

Private Citizen, Inc.
P.O. Box 233
Naperville, IL 60566
(800)CUT-JUNK
http://www.private-citizen.com

Privacy International
666 Pennsylvania Ave., SE, No. 301
Washington, D.C. 20003
(202) 483-1140
http://222.privacy.org/pi

Major credit card companies

American Express
Fraud Dept.
P.O. Box 53730
Phoenix, AZ 85073-3730
(800) 492-8468

MasterCard Global Service Center
Fraud Dept
P.O. Box 28468
St. Louis, MO 63146
(800) 307-7309
http://www.mastercard.com

Visa Assistance Center
Fraud Dept
P.O. Box 8999
San Francisco, CA 94128
(800) VISA911 (Hotline)
http://www.visa.com

Credit Bureaus

Equifax—www.equifax.com

> To order your report, call: 1-800-685-1111 or write:
> P.O. Box 740241, Atlanta, GA 30374-0241

> To report fraud, call: 1-800-525-6285 and write:
> P.O. Box 740241, Atlanta, GA 30374-0241

Experian—*www.experian.com*

To order your report, call: 1-888-EXPERIAN (397-3742) or write: P.O. Box 2104, Allen, TX 75013

To report fraud, call: 1-888-EXPERIAN (397-3742) and write: P.O. Box 9532, Allen, TX 75013

TransUnion—*www.transunion.com*

To order your report, call: 800-916-8800 or write: P.O. Box 1000, Chester, PA 19022.

To report fraud, call: 1-800-680-7289 and write: Fraud Victim Assistance Division, P.O. Box 6790, Fullerton, CA 92634

Banking Agencies

If you're having trouble getting your financial institution to help you resolve your banking- related identity theft problems, including problems with bank-issued credit cards, contact the agency with the appropriate jurisdiction. If you're not sure which agency has jurisdiction over your institution, call your bank or visit *www.ffiec.gov/nic/default.htm*.

Federal Deposit Insurance Corporation (FDIC)—
www.fdic.gov

The FDIC supervises state-chartered banks that are not members of the Federal Reserve System and insures deposits at banks and savings and loans. Call the FDIC Consumer Call Center at 1-800-934-3342; or write: Federal Deposit Insurance Corporation, Division of Compliance and Consumer Affairs, 550 17th Street, NW, Washington, DC 20429.

FDIC publications:

- *Classic Cons...And How to Counter Them*
- *Your Wallet: A Loser's Manual*
- *A Crook Has Drained Your Account. Who Pays?*

Federal Reserve System (Fed)—*www.federalreserve.gov*

The Fed supervises state-chartered banks that are members of the Federal Reserve System. Call: 202-452-3693; or write: Division of Consumer and Community Affairs, Mail Stop 801, Federal Reserve Board, Washington, DC 20551; or contact the Federal Reserve Bank in your area. The 12 Reserve Banks are located in Boston, New York, Philadelphia, Cleveland, Richmond, Atlanta, Chicago, St. Louis, Minneapolis, Kansas City, Dallas, and San Francisco.

National Credit Union Administration (NCUA)—
www.ncua.gov

The NCUA charters and supervises federal credit unions and insures deposits at federal credit unions and many state credit unions. Call: 703-518-6360; or write: Compliance Officer, National Credit Union Administration, 1775 Duke Street, Alexandria, VA 22314.

Office of the Comptroller of the Currency (OCC)—
www.occ.treas.gov

The OCC charters and supervises national banks. If the word "national" appears in the name of a bank, or the initials "N.A." follow its name, the OCC oversees its operations. Call: 1-800-613-6743 (business days 9:00 a.m. to 4:00 p.m. CST); fax: 713-336-4301; write: Customer Assistance Group, 1301 McKinney Street, Suite 3710, Houston, TX 77010.

OCC publications:

+ *Identity Theft and Pretext Calling Advisory Letter 2001-4*

+ *How to Avoid Becoming a Victim of Identity Theft*

Office of Thrift Supervision (OTS)—*www.ots.treas.gov*

The OTS is the primary regulator of all federal and many state-chartered thrift institutions, which include savings banks and savings and loan institutions. Call: 202-906-6000; or write: Office of Thrift Supervision, 1700 G Street, NW, Washington, DC 20552.

Other Federal agencies and departments

Federal Trade Commission (FTC)—*www.ftc.gov*

The FTC is the federal clearinghouse for complaints by victims of identity theft. Although the FTC does not have the authority to bring criminal cases, the Commission helps victims of identity theft by providing them with information to help resolve the financial and other problems that can result from identity theft. The FTC also may refer victim complaints to other appropriate government agencies and private organizations for action.

If you've been a victim of identity theft, file a complaint with the FTC by contacting the FTC's Identity Theft Hotline by telephone: toll-free 1-877-IDTHEFT (438-4338); TDD: 202-326-2502; by mail: Identity Theft Clearinghouse, Federal Trade Commission, 600 Pennsylvania Avenue, NW, Washington, DC 20580; or online: *www.consumer.gov/idtheft*.

FTC publications:

- *Avoiding Credit and Charge Card Fraud*

- *Credit and ATM Cards: What to Do If They're Lost or Stolen*

- *Credit Card Loss Protection Offers: They're The Real Steal*

- *Electronic Banking*

- *Fair Credit Billing*

- *Fair Credit Reporting*

- *Fair Debt Collection*

- *Getting Purse-onal: What To Do If Your Wallet or Purse Is Stolen*

- *How to Dispute Credit Report Errors*

- *Identity Crisis... What to Do If Your Identity Is Stolen*

- *Identity Thieves Can Ruin Your Good Name: Tips for Avoiding Identity Theft*

Department of Justice (DOJ)—*www.usdoj.gov*

The DOJ and its U.S. Attorneys prosecute federal identity theft cases. Information on identity theft is available at *www.usdoj.gov/criminal/fraud/idtheft.html.*

Federal Bureau of Investigation (FBI)—*www.fbi.gov*

The FBI is one of the federal criminal law enforcement agencies that investigates cases of identity theft. Local field offices are listed in the Blue Pages of your telephone directory.

FBI publication:

♦ *Protecting Yourself Against Identity Fraud*

Federal Communications Commission (FCC)—*www.fcc.gov*

The FCC regulates interstate and international communications by radio, television, wire, satellite and cable. The FCC's Consumer Information Bureau is a one-stop source for information, forms, applications and current issues before the FCC. Call: 1-888-CALL-FCC; TTY: 1-888-TELL-FCC; or write: Federal Communications Commission, Consumer Information Bureau, 445 12th Street, SW, Room 5A863, Washington, DC 20554. You can file complaints via the online complaint form at *www.fcc.gov,* or e-mail questions to fccinfo@fcc.gov.

Internal Revenue Service (IRS)—*www.treas.gov/irs/ci*

The IRS is responsible for administering and enforcing tax laws. If you believe someone has assumed your identity to file federal Income Tax Returns or to commit other tax fraud, call toll-free: 1-800-829-0433. For assistance to victims of identity theft schemes who are having trouble filing their correct returns, call the IRS Taxpayer Advocates Office, toll-free: 1-877-777- 4778.

U.S. Secret Service (USSS)—*www.treas.gov/usss*

The U.S. Secret Service is one of the federal law enforcement agencies that investigates financial crimes, which may include identity theft. Although the Secret Service generally investigates cases where the dollar loss is substantial, your information may provide evidence of a larger pattern of fraud requiring their involvement. Local field offices are listed in the Blue Pages of your telephone directory.

Social Security Administration (SSA)—*www.ssa.gov*

SSA may assign you a new SSN—at your request—if you continue to experience problems even after trying to resolve the problems resulting from identity theft. SSA field office employees work closely with victims of identity theft and third parties to collect the evidence needed to assign a new SSN in these cases.

The SSA Office of the Inspector General (SSA/OIG is one of the federal law enforcement agencies that investigates cases of identity theft. Direct allegations that an SSN has been stolen or misused to the SSA Fraud Hotline. Call: 1-800- 269-0271; fax: 410-597-0118; write: SSA Fraud Hotline, P.O. Box 17768, Baltimore, MD 21235; or e-mail: oig.hotline@ssa.gov

SSA publications:

- *SSA Fraud Hotline for Reporting Fraud*

- *Social Security When Someone Misuses Your Number (SSA Pub. No. 05-10064)*

- *Social Security: Your Number and Card (SSA Pub. No. 05-10002)*

U.S. Postal Inspection Service (USPIS)—
www.usps.gov/websites/depart/inspect

USPIS is the law enforcement arm of the U.S. Postal Service. USPIS has primary jurisdiction in all matters infringing on the integrity of the U.S. mail. You can locate the USPIS district office nearest you by calling your local post office or checking the list at the Website above.

U.S. Securities and Exchange Commission (SEC)—
www.sec.gov

The SEC's Office of Investor Education and Assistance serves investors who complain to the SEC about investment fraud or the mishandling of their investments by securities professionals. If you've experienced identity theft in connection with a securities transaction, you can file a complaint with the SEC by visiting the Complaint Center at www.sec.gov/complaint.shtml. Be sure to include as much detail as possible. If you do not have access to the Internet, write to the SEC at: SEC Office of Investor Education and Assistance, 450 Fifth Street, NW, Washington, DC 20549-0213, or call 202-942-7040.

U. S. Trustee (UST)—*www.usdoj.gov/ust*

If you believe someone has filed for bankruptcy using your name, write to the U.S. Trustee in the region where the bankruptcy was filed. A list of the U.S. Trustee's Regional Offices is available on the UST Website or check the Blue Pages of your phone book under U.S. Government Bankruptcy Administration. Your letter should describe the situation and provide proof of your identity. The U.S. Trustee, if appropriate, will make a criminal referral to criminal law enforcement authorities if you provide appropriate documentation to substantiate your claim. You also may want to file a complaint with the U.S. Attorney and/or the FBI in the city where the bankruptcy was filed.

The U.S. Trustee does not provide legal representation, legal advice or referrals to lawyers. That means you may need to hire an attorney to help convince the bankruptcy court that the filing is fraudulent. The U.S. Trustee does not provide consumers with copies of court documents. Those documents are available from the bankruptcy clerk's office for a fee.

Instructions for Completing the ID Theft Affidavit

To make certain that you do not become responsible for the debts incurred by the identity thief, you must provide proof that you didn't create the debt to each of the companies where accounts were opened or used in your name.

A working group composed of credit grantors, consumer advocates, and the Federal Trade Commission (FTC) developed this ID Theft Affidavit to help you report information to many companies using just one standard form. Use of this affidavit is optional. While many companies accept this affidavit, others require that you submit more or different forms. Before you send the affidavit, contact each company to find out if they accept it.

You can use this affidavit where a **new account** was opened in your name. The information will enable the companies to investigate the fraud and decide the outcome of your claim. (If someone made unauthorized charges to an **existing account**, call the company to find out what to do.)

This affidavit has two parts:

- ◆ **ID Theft Affidavit** is where you report general information about yourself and the theft.

♦ **Fraudulent Account Statement** is where you describe the fraudulent account(s) opened in your name. Use a separate Fraudulent Account Statement for each company you need to write to.

When you send the affidavit to the companies, attach copies (**NOT** originals) of any supporting documents (e.g., driver's license, police report) you have.

Before submitting your affidavit, review the disputed account(s) with family members or friends who may have information about the account(s) or access to them.

Complete this affidavit as soon as possible. Many creditors ask that you send it within two weeks of receiving it. Delaying could slow the investigation.

Be as accurate and complete as possible. You *may* choose not to provide some of the information requested. However, incorrect or incomplete information will slow the process of investigating your claim and absolving the debt. Please print clearly.

When you have finished completing the affidavit, mail a copy to each creditor, bank or company that provided the thief with the unauthorized credit, goods or services you describe. Attach to each affidavit a copy of the Fraudulent Account Statement with information only on accounts opened at the institution receiving the packet, as well as any other supporting documentation you are able to provide.

Send the appropriate documents to each company by certified mail, return receipt requested, so you can prove that it was received. The companies will review your claim and send you a written response telling you the outcome of their investigation. **Keep a copy of everything you submit for your records.**

If you cannot complete the affidavit, a legal guardian or someone with power of attorney may complete it for you. Except as noted, the information you provide will be used only by the company to process your affidavit, investigate the events you report and help stop further fraud. If this affidavit is requested in a lawsuit, the company might have to provide it to the requesting party.

Completing this affidavit does not guarantee that the identity thief will be prosecuted or that the debt will be cleared.

If you haven't already done so, report the fraud to the following organizations:

1. Each of the three **national consumer reporting agencies**. Ask each agency to place a "fraud alert" on your credit report, and send you a copy of your credit file. When you have completed your affidavit packet, you may want to send them a copy to help them investigate the disputed accounts.

> **Equifax Credit Information Services, Inc.**
> (800) 525-6285 (Hearing impaired call
> 1-800-255-0056 and ask the operator to call the
> Auto Disclosure Line at 1-800-685-1111 to obtain a
> copy of your report.)
> P.O. Box 740241
> Atlanta, GA 30374-0241
> *www.equifax.com*

> **Experian Information Solutions, Inc**.
> (888) 397-3742/ TDD (800) 972-0322
> P.O. Box 9530
> Allen, TX 75013
> *www.experian.com*

> **TransUnion**
> (800) 680-7289/ TDD (877) 553-7803
> Fraud Victim Assistance Division
> P.O. Box 6790
> Fullerton, CA 92634-6790
> *www.tuc.com*

2. The **fraud department at each creditor, bank, or utility/service** that provided the identity thief with unauthorized credit, goods or services. This would be a good time to find out if the company accepts this affidavit, and whether they require notarization or a copy of the police report.

3. Your local **police department**. Ask the officer to take a report and give you the report number or a copy of the report. When you have completed the affidavit packet, you may want to give your police department a copy to help them add to their report and verify the crime.

4. The FTC, which maintains the Identity Theft Data Clearinghouse—the federal government's centralized identity theft complaint database—and provides information to identity theft victims. You can call toll-free **1-877-ID-THEFT (1-877-438-4338)**, visit *www.consumer.gov/idtheft*, or send mail to:

> **Identity Theft Data Clearinghouse**
> Federal Trade Commission
> 600 Pennsylvania Avenue, NW
> Washington, DC 20580

The FTC collects complaints from identity theft victims and shares their information with law enforcement nationwide. This information also may be shared with other government agencies, consumer reporting agencies, and companies where the fraud was perpetrated to help resolve identity theft related problems.

Name _____ *Page 1*

Phone number _____

ID Theft Affidavit

Victim Information

1. My full legal name is

_____
(First)　　　　　　　(Middle)　　　　(Last)　　　(Jr., Sr., III)

2. (If different from above) When the events described in this affidavit took place, I was known as

_____
(First)　　　　　　　(Middle)　　　　(Last)　　　(Jr., Sr., III)

3. My date of birth is _____
　　　　　　　　　　　　　　　(day/month/year)

4. My social security number is_____

5. My driver's license or identification card state and number are_____

6. My current address is_____

　　City _____

　　State _____ Zip Code_____

7. I have lived at this address since_____
　　　　　　　　　　　　　　　　　　(month/year)

8. (If different from above) When the events described in this affidavit took place, my address was

　　_____

　　City _____

　　State _____ Zip Code_____

9. I lived at the address in #8 from
　　_____ until _____
　　　　(month/year)　　　　　　　(month/year)

10. My daytime telephone number is (____)_____

　　My evening telephone number is (____)_____

Name _____ *Page 2*

Phone number _____

How the Fraud Occurred
Check all that apply for items 11 - 17:

11. ☐ I did not authorize anyone to use my name or personal information to seek the money, credit, loans, goods or services described in this report.

12. ☐ I did not receive any benefit, money, goods or services as a result of the events described in this report.

13. ☐ My identification documents (for example, credit cards; birth certificate; driver's license; social security card; etc.) were ☐stolen ☐lost on or about _____.
    (day/month/year)

14. ☐ To the best of my knowledge and belief, the following person(s) used my information (for example, my name, address, date of birth, existing account numbers, social security number, mother's maiden name, etc.) or identification documents to get money, credit, loans, goods or services without my knowledge or authorization:

_____   _____

Name (if known)   Name (if known)

_____   _____

_____   _____

Address (if known)   Address (if known)

_____   _____

Phone number(s) (if known) Phone number(s) (if known)

_____   _____

additional information (if known) additional information (if known)

_____

_____

15. ☐ I do NOT know who used my information or identification documents to get money, credit, loans, goods or services without my knowledge or authorization.

16. ☐ Additional comments: (For example, description of the fraud, which documents or information were used or how the identity thief gained access to your information.)

_____

_____

_____

_____

_____

_____

_____

_____

_____

(Attach additional pages as necessary.)

Victim's Law Enforcement Actions

17. (check one) I ☐ am ☐ am not willing to assist in the prosecution of the person(s) who committed this fraud.

18. (check one) I ☐ am ☐ am not authorizing the release of this information to law enforcement for the purpose of assisting them in the investigation and prosecution of the person(s) who committed this fraud.

19. (check all that apply) I ☐ have ☐ have not reported the events described in this affidavit to the police or other law enforcement agency. The police ☐ did ☐ did not write a report.

Name _____

Phone number _____

In the event you have contacted the police or other law enforcement agency, please complete the following:

Agency #1_____

_____
Officer/Agency personnel taking report

_____
Date of report   Report Number, if any

_____
Phone number   E-mail address, if any

Agency #2_____

_____
Officer/Agency personnel taking report

_____
Date of report   Report Number, if any

_____
Phone number   E-mail address, if any

Documentation Checklist

Please indicate the supporting documentation you are able to provide to the companies you plan to notify. Attach copies (NOT originals) to the affidavit before sending it to the companies.

20. ☐ A copy of a valid government-issued photo-identification card (for example, your drivers license, state-issued ID card or your passport). If you are under 16 and don't have a photo-ID, you may submit a copy of your birth certificate or a copy of your official school records showing your enrollment and place of residence.

Name _____ *Page 4*

Phone number_____

21. ☐ Proof of residency during the time the disputed bill occurred, the loan was made or the other event took place (for example, a rental/lease agreement in your name, a copy of a utility bill or a copy of an insurance bill).

22. ☐ A copy of the report you filed with the police or sheriff's department. If you are unable to obtain a report or report number from the police, please indicate that in Item 19. Some companies only need the report number, not a copy of the report. You may want to check with each company.

Signature
I declare under penalty of perjury that the information I have provided in this affidavit is true and correct to the best of my knowledge.

_____   _____
(signature)   (date signed)

Knowingly submitting false information on this form could subject you to criminal prosecution for perjury.

_____

(Notary)
(Check with each company. Creditors sometimes require notarization. If they do not, please have one witness (non-relative) sign below that you completed and signed this affidavit.)
Witness:

_____   _____
(signature)   (printed name)

_____   _____
(date)   (telephone number)

Name _____ *Page 5*

Phone number _____

Fradulent Account Statement

Completing this Statement

- Make as many copies of this page as you need. **Complete a separate page for each company you're notifying and only send it to that company.** Include a copy of your signed affidavit.

- List only the account(s) you're disputing with the company receiving this form. **See the example below.**

- If a collection agency sent you a statement, letter or notice about the fraudulent account, attach a copy of that document (**NOT** the original).

I declare (check all that apply):

☐ As a result of the event(s) described in the ID Theft Affidavit, the following account(s) was/were opened at your company in my name without my knowledge, permission or authorization using my personal information or identifying documents:

Creditor Name/ Address (company that opened the account or provided the goods or services)	Account Number	Type of unauthorized credit/goods/ services provided by creditor (if known)	Date issued or opened (if known)	Amount/ Value provided (the amount charged or the cost of the goods/ services)
Example Example Bank 22 Main Street Columbus, Ohio 22722	012345	Auto loan	01/05/02	$25,500.00

☐ During the time of the accounts described above, I had the following account open with your company:

Billing name_____

Billing address_____

Account number_____

1-877-IDTHEFT (1.877.438.4338)
www.consumer.gov/idtheft

Endnotes

Introduction

[1] "Anatomy of an ID Fraud." *Kiplinger's Personal Finance.* March 2001. <www.kiplinger.com/ma...archives/2001/March/managing/idfraud.html> (15 October 2002).

Chapter 1

[1] Attorney General John Ashcroft, transcript of remarks at Identity Theft Press Conference held with FTC Trade Commission Chairman Timothy J. Muris and Senator Diane Feinstein, 2 May 2002. p. 5.

[2] CALPIRG (The California Public Interest Research Group) and the Privacy Rights Clearinghouse. "Nowhere to Turn: Victims Speak Out on Identity Theft, A Survey of Identity Theft Victims and Recommendations for Reform" (report). May 2000. p. 1.

[3] Sean B. Hoar, US Department of Justice, Executive Office for United States Attorneys. "Identity Theft: The Crime of the New Millennium." *USA Bulletin*, March 2001, Vol. 49, No. 2. p. 1.

[4] Jonathan J. Rusch. "Making a Federal Case of Identity Theft: The Department of Justice's Role in Identity Theft Prevention and Enforcement." <www.usdoj.gov:80/criminal/fraud/fedcase_idtheft.html> (15 October 2002). p. 1.

[5] Department of Justice. "Identity Theft and Fraud." <www.usdoj.gov:80/criminal/fraud/text/idtheft.html> (15 October 2002). p. 2.

[6] U.S. Department of Justice, Office of Justice. "Programs Financial Crimes." National Victim Assistance Academy 2001 Text, Chapter 16. p. 9.

[7] Ibid.

[8] Interview by author, April 2, 2002.

[9] Sean B. Hoar, US Department of Justice, Executive Office for United States Attorneys. "Identity Theft: The Crime of the New Millennium." *USA Bulletin*, March 2001, Vol. 49, No. 2. p. 1.

[10] Ibid. p. 2.

[11] CALPIRG (The California Public Interest Research Group) and the Privacy Rights Clearinghouse. "Nowhere to Turn: Victims Speak Out on Identity Theft, A Survey of Identity Theft Victims and Recommendations for Reform" (report). May 2000. p. 1.

[12] Ibid. p. 2.

[13] Federal Trade Commission. "ID Theft: When Bad Things Happen to Your Good Name." September 2002. <www.ftc.gov/bcp/conline/pubs/credit/idtheft/htm> (15 October 2002). p. 3.

[14] Ibid. p. 4.

[15] Attorney General John Ashcroft, transcript of remarks at Identity Theft Press Conference held with FTC Trade Commission Chairman Timothy J. Muris and Senator Diane Feinstein, 2 May 2002.

[16] U.S. Department of Justice, US Attorney's Office, Southern District of Texas. Fact Sheet: "Identity Theft Prosecution and Prevention." May 2002. p. 2.

Chapter 3

[1] Ramer, Holly, "Professor Killer Hit with Conspiracy", Associated Press, May 29, 2002.

[2] Author interview of Judge Roger Luebs, former Riverside County (CA) Deputy District Attorney, April 2, 2002.

[3] U.S. Department of Justice Press Release, October 20, 1999.

[4] Jonathan J. Rusch. "Making a Federal Case of Identity Theft: The Department of Justice's Role in Identity Theft Prevention and Enforcement." <www.usdoj.gov:80/criminal/fraud/fedcase_idtheft.html> (15 October 2002). p. 2.

[5] Jane E. Limprecht, Executive Office for U.S. Trustees, Department of Justice. "Fresh Start or False Start?—Identity Theft in Bankruptcy Cases." <www.usdoj.gov:80/ust/press/articles/idtheftfinal.html> (15 October 2002). p. 1.

[6] Statement for the Record by Grant D. Ashley, Assistant Director, Criminal Investigation Division, Federal Bureau of Investigation, on Preserving the Integrity of Social Security Numbers and Preventing their Misuse by Terrorist and Identity Thieves, before the House Ways and Means Committee, Subcommittee on Social Security, 19 September 2002.

[7] Mieszkowski, Katherine, "Wanted: Your Name and Number", Salon.com, October 2, 2001.

[8] Ibid.

[9] Statement for the Record by Dennis M Lormel, Chief, Terrorist Financial Review Group, Federal Bureau of Investigation, before the Senate Judiciary Committee, Subcommittee on Technology, Terrorism and Government Information. Hearing on S2541, "The Identity Theft Penalty Enhancement Act," 9 July 2002. p. 2.

[10] Ibid.

[11] Murphy, Belkin, The Boston Globe, Jan. 31, 2002.

[12] Hanley, Robert, "Fugitive in phony-papers scam nabbed," New York Times, August 21, 2002.

[13] Parry, Wayne, "Sept. 11 Fake ID Suspect Flees U.S.," Associated Press, Jul 31, 2002.

[14] Beth Givens, Director, Privacy Rights Clearinghouse. "Identity Theft: How it Happens, Its Impact on Victims and Legislative Solutions" (written testimony for U.S. Senate Judiciary Subcommittee on Technology, Terrorism and Government Information), 12 July 2000. p. 5.

[15] Baird, Woody, I.D. Worker Burned to Death, Associated Press, March 5, 2002.

[16] Bill Dries. "Patrol Says Examiner's Death Not Due to Crash." *Memphis Commercial Appeal*, 6 March 2002, News, A1.

[17] Ibid.

[18] Winter, Carl, "New Jersey Indicts 36 in State Document Fraud Probe", Reuters, June 24, 2002.

[19] "FBI hunts men in alleged visa scam", The Press-enterprise, July 9, 2002.

[20] "Russian mob may have infiltrated university computers," Associated Press, June 18, 2002.

[21] Sullivan, Bob, "Inside a Net Extortion Ring", MSNBC.com, June 20, 2002.

[22] "Anatomy of an ID Fraud." *Kiplinger's Personal Finance.* March 2001. <www.kiplinger.com/ma...archives/2001/March/managing/idfraud.html> (15 October 2002). p. 6.

[23] Reiter, Luke, "Are You an Identity Theft Victim?", TechTV, January 10, 2000.

[24] "New twist on ID theft", Bottom Line Personal, Vol. 23, No. 15, August 1, 2002. p. 9.

[25] Jonathan J. Rusch. "Making a Federal Case of Identity Theft: The Department of Justice's Role in Identity Theft Prevention and Enforcement." <www.usdoj.gov:80/criminal/fraud/fedcase_idtheft.html> (15 October 2002). p. 1.

[26] Sean B. Hoar, US Department of Justice, Executive Office for United States Attorneys. "Identity Theft: The Crime of the New Millennium." *USA Bulletin*, March 2001, Vol. 49, No. 2. pp. 6-7.

[27] "Worker accused of selling colleagues' Ids online," by Jacob H. Fries, New York Times, March 2, 2002.

[28] Office of New York State Attorney General Eliot Spitzer. "State worker charged in massive identity theft scam" (press release, July 17, 2001).

[29] Department of Justice press release, May 2, 2002. <www.usdoj.gov:80/usao/mie/pr/sweep2002/html> (15 October 2002).

[30] Michael Bedan. "ID-theft ring broken." *Rocky Mountain News*, 10 October 2002.

[31] Author interview of Judge Roger Luebs, former Riverside County (CA) Deputy District Attorney.

[32] Bartholomew Sullivan and Bill Dries. "ID Theft Sentence Confines Preacher." *Memphis Commercial Appeal*, 5 January 2002, Metro, B1.

[33] "Memphis Police Officer Charged in Identity Theft Scheme." *Memphis Commercial Appeal*, 4 May 2002, Metro, B2, Final ed.

[34] Bill Dries. "Chief ID Thief Gets New One From Judge-Jailbird." *Memphis Commercial Appeal*, 20 December 2001, Metro, B1.

[35] Stokley, Sandra, "Woman pleads guilty to stealing truck", The Press-Enterprise, May 2, 2002, p. B3.

[36] Stokley, Sandra, "Suspect who missed court date arrested," The Press-Enterprise, April 25, 2002, p. B5.

[37] Ho, David, "FTC Warns on Telemarketing Scheme", Associated Press, June 25, 2002.

[38] "IRS warns of scheme to steal identity and financial data," IRS News Release No. IR-2002-55, May 1, 2002.

Chapter 4

[1] Newman, John, Q., Identity Theft: The Cybercrime of the Millenium, Loompanics Unlimited, p. 11.

[2] CALPIRG (The California Public Interest Research Group) and the Privacy Rights Clearinghouse. "Nowhere to Turn: Victims Speak Out on Identity Theft, A Survey of Identity Theft Victims and Recommendations for Reform" (report). May 2000. p. 3.

[3] General Accounting Office. "Identity Theft: Prevalence and Cost Appears to be Growing (GAO-02-363)." March 2002. p. 8.

[4] CALPIRG (The California Public Interest Research Group) and the Privacy Rights Clearinghouse. "Nowhere to Turn: Victims Speak Out on Identity Theft, A Survey of Identity Theft Victims and Recommendations for Reform" (report). May 2000. p. 1.

[5] "Ford Credit Warns of Identity Theft," Associated Press, May 16, 2002.

[6] Sean B. Hoar, US Department of Justice, Executive Office for United States Attorneys. "Identity Theft: The Crime of the New Millennium." *USA Bulletin*, March 2001, Vol. 49, No. 2. p. 3.

[7] Excerpts of testimony of Michael J. Mansfield, Assistant District Attorney and Chief, Economic Crimes Bureau, Queens County District Attorney's Office, before the U.S. House of Representatives Committee on Small Business, Subcommittee on Regulatory Reform and Network Reduction.

[8] "On-line Fraud and Crime: Are Consumers Safe?", statement of Bruce Swartz, Deputy Assistant Attorney General, Criminal Division, Department of Justice, at a hearing before the Subcommittee on Commerce, Trade, and Consumer Protection, House Committee on Energy and Commerce, May 23, 2001.

Chapter 5

[1] CALPIRG (The California Public Interest Research Group) and the Privacy Rights Clearinghouse. "Nowhere to Turn: Victims Speak Out on Identity Theft, A Survey of Identity Theft Victims and Recommendations for Reform" (report). May 2000. p. 2.

[2] Beth Givens, Director, Privacy Rights Clearinghouse. "Identity Theft: How it Happens, Its Impact on Victims and Legislative Solutions" (written testimony for U.S. Senate Judiciary Subcommittee on Technology, Terrorism and Government Information), 12 July 2000. p. 2.

[3] "Woods Says he was a Victim of Identity Theft", Associated Press, December 20, 2000).

[4] Associated Press. "Man Faces Jordan ID Theft Charge." 5 October 2002.

[5] Jane E. Limprecht, Executive Office for U.S. Trustees, Department of Justice. "Fresh Start or False Start?—Identity Theft in Bankruptcy Cases." <www.usdoj.gov:80/ust/press/articles/idtheftfinal.html> (15 October 2002). p. 1.

[6] Ibid.

[7] Ibid.

[8] Statement for the Record by Grant D. Ashley, Assistant Director, Criminal Investigation Division, Federal Bureau of Investigation, on Preserving the Integrity of Social Security Numbers and Preventing their Misuse by Terrorist and Identity Thieves, before the House Ways and Means Committee, Subcommittee on Social Security, 19 September 2002.

[9] Stabile, Tom, "Identity Thief preys on Cardozo Students", National Jurist, January, 2002.

[10] Department of Justice press release, May 2, 2002. <www.usdoj.gov:80/usao/mie/pr/sweep2002/html> (15 October 2002). p. 1.

[11] "Identity Thieves Get Online", CBSNEWS.com, March 12, 2002.

[12] Author interview with Judge Roger Luebs, former Riverside County (CA) Deputy District Attorney, April 2, 2002.

[13] Statement for the Record by Grant D. Ashley, Assistant Director, Criminal Investigation Division, Federal Bureau of Investigation, on Preserving the Integrity of Social Security Numbers and Preventing their Misuse by Terrorist and Identity Thieves, before the House Ways and Means Committee, Subcommittee on Social Security, 19 September 2002.

[14] Department of Justice press release, May 2, 2002. <www.usdoj.gov:80/usao/mie/pr/sweep2002/html> (15 October 2002), p. 1.

[15] Gail Appleson. "Busboy Admits Stealing Data of U.S. Rich and Famous." "Oddly Enough," Reuters.com, 4 October 2002.

[16] Ibid.

[17] Is There Another You?" House of Representatives, Committee on Commerce, Subcommittee on Telecommunications, Trade, and Consumer Protection, joint with Subcommittee on Finance and Hazardous Materials, Washington, D.C., April 22, 1999.

[18] Author interview with Judge Roger Luebs, former Riverside County (CA) Deputy District Attorney, April 2, 2002.

[19] "Police Nab Corporate Identity Thieves," TechTV, October 12, 1998.

Chapter 6

[1] Department of Justice. "Identity Theft and Fraud." <www.usdoj.gov:80/criminal/fraud/text/idtheft.html> (15 October 2002), pp. 5-7.

[2] Hopper, D. Ian, "New Web site lets credit card holders check to see if numbers stolen," Associated Press, June 26, 2002.

[3] "Man Gamed ID System Using Surprisingly Little Information", Associated Press, July 14, 2002.

Chapter 7

[1] Attorney General John Ashcroft, transcript of remarks at Identity Theft Press Conference held with FTC Trade Commission Chairman Timothy J. Muris and Senator Diane Feinstein, 2 May 2002, p. 4.

[2] Jonathan J. Rusch. "Making a Federal Case of Identity Theft: The Department of Justice's Role in Identity Theft Prevention and Enforcement." <www.usdoj.gov:80/criminal/fraud/fedcase_idtheft.html> (15 October 2002), p. 2.

[3] Jane E. Limprecht, Executive Office for U.S. Trustees, Department of Justice. "Fresh Start or False Start?—Identity Theft in Bankruptcy Cases." <www.usdoj.gov:80/ust/press/articles/idtheftfinal.html> (15 October 2002), p. 2.

[4] Ibid.

[5] Federal Trade Commission. Prepared statement on The Identity Theft Penalty Enhancement Act of 2002 (by Howard Beales, Director of the Bureau of Consumer Protection, FTC), before The Subcommittee on Technology, Terrorism and Government Information of the Senate Judiciary Committee, 9 July 2002.

[6] General Accounting Office. "Identity Theft: Prevalence and Cost Appears to be Growing (GAO-02-363)." March 2002. p. 8.

[7] Federal Trade Commission. "A Summary of Your Rights Under the Fair Credit Reporting Act." <www.ftc.gov/bcp/conline/edcams/fcra/summary.html> (15 October 2002).

[8] Federal Trade Commission Facts for Consumers. "Fair Credit Billing." <www.ftc.gov/bcp/conline/pubs/credit/fcb.html> (15 October 2002), pp. 1-2.

[9] Federal Trade Commission Facts for Consumers. "Electronic Banking." <www.ftc.gov/bcp/conline/pubs/credit/elbank.html> (15 October 2002), p. 2.

[10] Press release from office of Congressman Jim Moran, May 1, 2002.

Chapter 8

[1] "Identity Theft: What to do if it happens to you", a joint publication of the Privacy Rights Clearinghouse and CALPIRG, p. 1.

[2] U.S. Department of Justice, Office of Justice. "Programs Financial Crimes." National Victim Assistance Academy 2001 Text, Chapter 16. p. 10.

Index

About the Author

Robert Hammond is the author of *Repair Your Own Credit*, *Life After Debt*, *Credit Secrets*, and *Super Privacy*. He has a degree in Psychology and Sociology and studied law at Western State University in Fullerton, California.

Hammond has worked as an arbitrator for the Better Business Bureau, an investigator for the Fair Housing Council, and consultant to Consumer Credit Counseling Services of the Inland Empire and was instrumental in establishing Riverside (CA) County's Alternative Dispute Resolution Program. A highly sought-after public speaker, Hammond is a frequent guest on radio and television talk shows throughout the country.

He is currently working on a novel and film adaptation about identity theft, organized crime and international terrorism.